The big lesson of the last few year: held—that far too many people w news and spiritually shaped by their social media. That's part of why I am thankful that my friend Daniel Im wrote this book. He recognizes the problem, but he does more—he analyzes it with precision and offers indispensable insight into how to move forward for evangelism, discipleship, and preaching. The title is right. We have an opportunity; let's seize it!

ED STETZER, PhD, dean of Talbot School of Theology

In *The Discipleship Opportunity*, author Daniel Im confronts head-on the current church realities of declining attendance, political conflict, and racial tension. In response, Im provides a framework that moves beyond the Sunday-gathering model and shows leaders how to develop genuine disciples that meet Jesus on a deep and meaningful level. The remarkable insights in *The Discipleship Opportunity* have the power to ignite a movement where God's people take His love into the world in an authentic, life-changing way!

DAVE FERGUSON, coauthor of *B.L.E.S.S.: 5 Everyday Ways to Love Your Neighbor and Change the World*

In a world rocked by pandemics, wars, and weather events, Daniel Im's *The Discipleship Opportunity* is the guide for Christian leaders in this post-everything era. Im's book is punchy, insightful, and practical. Whether you're a rookie or a seasoned leader, Im's wisdom will equip you to lead and challenge others along the discipleship pathway.

SAM CHAN, lead mentor at EvQ School of Evangelism (a ministry of City Bible Forum) and author of *How to Talk about Jesus (without Being That Guy)*

Daniel Im has long been a significant voice in church planting and mission circles. Now he brings a lot of experience leading a generative church network in the increasingly secular Canadian context into the equation. The result is a book with gravitas and insight for our times.

ALAN HIRSCH, author of numerous books on missional churches, spirituality, and leadership; cofounder of Movement Leaders Collective and Forge Mission Training Network

Over the last several decades, church leaders have packed a lot of ideas, assumptions, methods, and mindsets into their travel bag to accomplish our God-given mission to make disciples. The basic equipment we were commissioned to carry by the Leader of the missional journey has become weighted down with ill-fitting garments and accoutrements. Daniel has done the hard work of unpacking the cultural extras, leaving the essentials for traveling lightly. He has done so not with a theorist's ideology but as a practitioner. This book is refreshing—and, frankly, relieving! A must-read for every weary traveler.

DR. TAMMY DUNAHOO, executive dean of Portland Seminary at George Fox University

Daniel Im has provided a gentle overview of a better pathway for discipleship in the local church. This book demonstrates the insights and skill of a pastor who is focused on disciplemaking. Recommended for senior pastors and leadership teams.

BOBBY HARRINGTON, author and point leader of Discipleship.org and Renew.org

"Kindly confrontational" was the phrase that came to mind as I read *The Discipleship Opportunity*. In this book, Daniel challenges us to face our assumptions about how a church grows. With practical ideas and a simple tool, he shares concrete steps every church pastor can take to minister to the people in their church and beyond.

JESSIE CRUICKSHANK, founder of Whoology and author of *Ordinary Discipleship*

Serving and leading in the local church in our post-everything world feels eminently complex. We need wise guides to help us down the path toward better days ahead. My friend Daniel Im's new book is such a guide. Leaning on years of pastoral and leadership experience, along with his distinctive warmth, humility, and deep love for the local church and its leaders, *The Discipleship Opportunity* is inspiring, accessible, and, maybe most importantly, a practically helpful and applicable tool for church leaders in almost any context. This is a book for our time and for the seasons ahead.

JAY Y. KIM, pastor and author of *Analog Christian*

What does it actually mean to be a pastor in a post-pandemic world? What does it mean to be the church in a post-everything society? Pastor and author Daniel Im is seeking to answer those questions. But rather than giving us a post-pandemic book, or offering a new hot take on church models, Im provides church leaders with hope, guidance, and a beautiful Jesus-way forward.

With a deep love for his audience, the church, and Jesus, Im has managed to create more than a playbook for discipleship; his words breathe new life into dry bones.

AUBREY SAMPSON, author of *Known* and *The Louder Song*, church planter, teaching pastor, and coleader of Chicagoland's New Thing Network for female church planters

Too often we try to lead churches with erroneous assumptions and misguided practices when what we really need is to trust the Holy Spirit. Nevertheless, we must work to develop a strong aptitude and strong attitude for pastoring and learn to never give up. In *The Discipleship Opportunity*, Daniel Im reveals many ways to engage the sleepers, seekers, and consumers in your church— how to entice and equip them on the discipleship path. He charts the promise Jesus makes to us all to live "life to the full."

KYLE IDLEMAN, senior pastor of Southeast Christian Church and author of *When Your Way Isn't Working*

Daniel Im sees where we need to go as leaders and presents us with a path to get there. In his latest book, *The Discipleship Opportunity*, he offers a compelling, practical, timely, and biblical framework for leading, discipling, and preaching differently yet effectively in today's post-everything, complicated world.

BRAD LOMENICK, author of *H3 Leadership* and *The Catalyst Leader*, former president of Catalyst

Provocative! This book, a must-read for any church leader, is the first book to give context and strategy to the post-pandemic "future church." Daniel not only challenges the status quo but also provides practicable solutions for your church! Read this book, go through it with your team, and implement its recommendations.

SEAN MORGAN, founder of The Ascent Leader

There is an invitation that awaits us. Even after all humanity has endured, Daniel Im has a way with words and a Kingdom vision to change adversity into opportunity. In Daniel's latest book, *The Discipleship Opportunity*, he bravely guides you in such thoughtful and accessible ways to better reach, preach to, and disciple your people in the way of Jesus. A must-read!

STEVE CARTER, pastor and author of *Grieve, Breathe, Receive*

There's no doubt about it—our world is very different now than it used to be, which means the mission field of *every* church has changed as well. Rather than blaming our post-pandemic, post-Christian culture, we need to embrace the opportunity to revisit how we engage the gospel mission. It really *is* an opportunity. It's a privilege. It's our calling. By the time you finish this book, I hope my friend Daniel Im will have convinced you it's time to revisit how to lead, teach, and engage the mission of helping people meet and follow Jesus.

TONY MORGAN, founder and lead strategist of The Unstuck Group

THE
DISCIPLESHIP
OPPORTUNITY

Leading a
Great-Commission
Church in a
Post-Everything
World

DANIEL IM

A NavPress resource published in alliance
with Tyndale House Publishers

NavPress.com

30	29	28	27	26	25	24
7	6	5	4	3	2	1

To all the spiritually blind, asleep, and dead:

"Awake, O sleeper,

rise up from the dead,

and Christ will give you light."

EPHESIANS 5:14, NLT

Contents

Introduction

THE SILENCE WAS DEAFENING IN THE NEARLY EMPTY ROOM.

I stood on the stage with my head held high and my wife next to me, ready to accept the challenge of being the lead pastor of a local church in the middle of a global pandemic.

When our congregation was asked, "Will you embrace Jesus as Lord afresh today?" there was no response. And then when our denominational leader asked, "Will you pray for the Ims and hold Daniel in his office of lead pastor in high regard? Will you be slow to criticize and quick to encourage?" there was no sound. No chorus of amens, no indication of agreement, and no verbal affirmation.

As I stood in front of the video cameras to affirm my pastoral calling and share my first words as lead pastor,[1] I was desperately hoping that my family and the few "essential workers" in the building weren't the only ones listening. Did our congregation respond positively? Or had they just left the service on as background noise while they were making breakfast or doing laundry? There was no way to know.

This wasn't how I'd envisioned my installation service would go when we left Nashville and moved back to Edmonton to pastor Beulah Alliance Church. If this global pandemic—and the politicization of it—wasn't enough to baptize me by fire into my new role, my dad died a week after my installation. Then one of our beloved pastors died. Then a suicide shook our congregation. It was around this time that our church started both losing and welcoming people at such a flurried pace that it was hard to know where we stood.

How was I supposed to lead? How was I supposed to fulfill the pledge I'd made to our church to lead and disciple people to know Jesus deeply and experience being known by Him fully?

THESE CHALLENGES ARE NOT NEW

Most pastors and ministry leaders would agree that leading a church through the pandemic years was tough. Every church leader has their own story of the struggles they faced during those dark and lonely days—pastoring their congregation through fear of a contagious illness, caring for sick congregants, navigating pandemic politics, making decisions about building occupancy and mask policies, and dealing with church members who didn't agree with their decisions.

Many of us found ourselves in situations that were highly

unsettling, and everything came at us so fast. We may have heard our church members say things like these:

"I can't believe they actually said that."
"But that's not what I meant!"
"My goodness . . . they left too?"
"I just don't know what to do anymore."

If any of this sounds familiar, I want to tell you that I'm sorry and I feel your pain. For a while now it has felt like we've been strapped in on a relational, emotional, and spiritual roller coaster that has left many of us reeling from this adrenaline-spiking ride.

Just to be clear: This book is not about the pandemic and its effects on the church (or church leaders). The challenges we are facing are not new. The truth is that for years, much of the church has been slowly forgetting her identity; the pandemic simply accelerated what was already happening underneath the surface.

THE PATH FORWARD

In a quest to regain a semblance of normalcy, some people believe that the path forward is backward—to get back to the way things used to be. While that strategy might work for some things, it won't work for churches in this season.

One thing I've realized is that before 2020, instead of teaching our people how to live like the Light of the World, we let them settle with the shadow of *our* light. Instead of prioritizing disciplemaking in our church, we elevated attendance as our key metric for success. And instead of equipping our people to do the work of an evangelist, we did it for them (and aren't some of us *still* doing this today?). In other words, the pandemic revealed what was already true of us—we're not as good at discipleship as we thought we were.

Meanwhile, our culture has become more divisive, political, tribal, indifferent, and impatient than any of us can remember it being before. Our world has changed, and people have changed; as a result, the way we lead in the church must change. The church's approach to discipleship, evangelism, and preaching needs to look different today than it did yesterday.

As the lead pastor of a multigenerational, multiethnic, and multicampus church, I've been wrestling with the following question: How can we navigate through today's challenging culture and become a stronger, healthier, and more on-mission church?

That's where the discipleship framework presented in this book comes into play. It will equip and empower you to lead, evangelize, disciple, and preach differently in today's post-everything world—since we literally seem to be post-*everything*! Post-pandemic, post-truth, post-Christian, and post-_____ (fill in the blank).

In part 1 of this book, you will learn how to identify the shifts you must make in your ministry to thrive in this new world. This book's discipleship framework is not prescriptive, so you're not going to find a time-bound and ministry-specific model offered here. And I'm not selling you a program or curriculum, either. You'll learn that the model of ministry most churches have followed since the 1950s was never binary. The people in your church aren't solely Christian or non-Christian—the situation is more nuanced than that. Accordingly, the ministry framework described in this book identifies the discipleship needs of four kinds of people sitting in our pews.

In part 2, we will dive deep into each quadrant of the framework to understand the four different types of people in your church and what it will take to

- reach the spiritually sleeping and dead in your community,
- disciple your people to know Jesus deeply and experience being known by Him fully, and
- preach in today's post-everything world.

This book is a guide to help you chart a fruitful and hope-filled path forward for your church. The church isn't dead! This is hard for some pastors to believe, especially if their church isn't as full as it used to be, or if it's hard to tell who has left versus who watches services online.

But Jesus never said that He *might* build a few churches—if the conditions are ideal, or if He has the right leaders in place. No, Jesus said that He *will* build His church, and that nothing and no one can or will ever overpower, overcome, or prevail against her—not even the gates of hell (Matthew 16:18).

Jesus is the master builder and the cornerstone. He is the King of kings and the Lord of lords. And we, the church, are His beloved bride. So no matter what comes our way, Jesus will always prevail and conquer—in His perfect timing—because He loves us, He cares for us, and He gave Himself for us.

This means that regardless of what has happened to your church, or what is happening right now, He's got this. He is your shepherd and defender. He is protecting and leading you with His rod and His staff. And He will renew your life and your church by leading you along the right path for His name's sake (Psalm 23).

If we want to be healthier, stronger, and better able to fulfill Jesus' command to make disciples of all nations, we need a new discipleship strategy. This is the wonderful opportunity before us.

Let's get started!

PART ONE

DIAGNOSING THE PROBLEM
AND SHIFTING OUR
APPROACH

Preparing

the Way

for the

Discipleship

Opportunity

CHAPTER 1

THE ASSUMPTIONS WE CAN'T AFFORD TO MAKE

If it does not work to the glory of God

and the extension of Christ's church,

throw it away and get something which does.

DONALD A. MCGAVRAN,
GOD, MAN, AND CHURCH GROWTH

"DO YOU KNOW WHY I STOPPED YOU?" the police officer asked.

My heart was racing. I could feel my body tensing up.

As I handed over my license and registration, I thought, *Why is he asking me this? I didn't do anything wrong! The light was green, and I think I was going the speed limit (or slightly above . . . but isn't that what everyone does?).*

This was my first time seeing flashing lights directed at me. I had just gotten my driver's license earlier that year. So when the officer asked me this question, I didn't know how to answer. I was scared, nervous, embarrassed, frustrated, and bewildered—one after another and at the same time. After all, I hated getting in trouble. And then, after what seemed like an eternity (but was probably only a few seconds), just as I was starting to say something that sounded like a sentence, he exclaimed: "You cut me off!"

I wasn't expecting *that*. I immediately blurted out, "I cut you off?"

"Yeah, you cut me off back there!" And then, pointing to my mirrors, he continued: "You can't trust these things. You have to check your blind spots."

Something I have learned in my almost twenty years as a pastor is that blind spots don't exist just on the road. We all have blind spots in our leadership—and we always will. They affect the way we lead and how our churches are run. And though we'll never be able to get rid of them, it's important that we check them regularly.

Unfortunately, checking our blind spots is not as simple as looking over our shoulder. As church leaders, we must learn how to uncover what we've been blind to within our churches. My prayer and hope is that this book will help you discern the blind spots in your unique context, just as it has for me.

UNPACK YOUR ASSUMPTIONS

You're busy. I get it. I have a stack of books I want to read, another sermon I need to write, congregants who are asking to meet, and more unread emails than I care to admit. So if you want to skip this chapter and flip to the framework part of the book, I understand.

But here's why you shouldn't: We must unpack our assumptions if we want to see our blind spots. And blind spots—when left unchecked—can lead to distressing and potentially disastrous consequences for you and your church.

As a church leader, you've likely found yourself wondering, *Why was giving down last week? Why was attendance up? Why aren't people growing deeper in their faith? Why didn't people laugh at my joke, and what can I do about it?* Your answers to each of these questions, except the one about the joke (sorry, I can't help you there), aren't as straightforward as they might seem.

Because we're living in a day and age when everyone seems to know *something* about *everything* (or at least pretends to), it's easy to assume that we already know the answers to these questions. In fact, your assumption might even be that *you* came up with that brilliant idea on how to break the two-hundred barrier or finally close the back door of your church!

Now, even if you did come up with those ideas yourself, would it be accurate to say that those ideas were *truly* yours? That they were 100 percent original to you?

Of course not! The best ideas are a synthesis of other ideas, so if you assume that the way you are leading is *completely* original to you, you probably have more blind spots than you realize.

After all, unless we consciously do otherwise, don't we teach the way that we've been taught? Lead the way that we've been led? Parent the way that we've been parented? And love the way that we've been loved? At least to some extent?

Sure, Daniel, you may be thinking, *but that doesn't help me disciple people well. I still have lots of questions.* Perhaps you're asking yourself, *How do I reach the spiritually sleeping and spiritually dead in my community? How do I disciple people to know Jesus deeply and experience being known by Him fully? And how do I preach in this post-everything world?*

To answer these questions, we must first unpack the assumptions behind them. Before making a lane change, we need to shoulder-check the thought patterns that have been driving our models of ministry. This will help us avoid repeating past mistakes—and perpetuating ineffective and outdated practices.

Assumption #1: "Of Course, Church"

A paradigm that has been highly influential in the Western church is the church growth movement,[1] which began in the 1950s. It was a movement of theologians and practitioners who advocated the idea that it is God's will for every church to grow. If your church isn't growing, the thinking went, then you must be doing something wrong.

After surveying the dominant thought leaders, books, paradigms, and principles of the church growth movement, I uncovered two of its foundational assumptions that continue to affect church practice today. The first is the assumption that everyone is still generally interested in the church.

The founder of the church growth movement, Donald A. McGavran, taught that "today there is unprecedented receptivity to the message of Christ. Today people are more winnable; the nations, the tribes, and the castes of the world are more responsive to the gospel than they have ever been before. There is no need to believe that pessimism and indifference outweigh God's grace."[2] The church growth movement perpetuated the assumption that if you have the right programs, meet the right felt needs, and are in the right location, then of course people will come. Of course, church!

I even heard one "expert" advocating the view that a church

should function like a car dealership. Your weekend worship service is the showroom floor where you display and sell the product, which is Christianity. The brands and models of cars that you sell are based on your denomination, tradition, worship style, and church model. And—since the bread and butter of every dealership is their service department—it's the church's programs that keep people coming back.

While I could spend the rest of this book deconstructing how grossly inappropriate and inaccurate this analogy is, I'll keep my observations to this: The church is not a business. We don't sell Christianity. We don't market Jesus. And we don't need to be the best show in town. The church is the holy bride of Christ, and we need to treat her with the love and respect she deserves. She is not a product that can be bought or sold.

Even though most church growth experts would likely agree with those observations, the assumption "of course, church" has nevertheless been shaping church practice for decades. Here are four misguided ways it continues to do so.

- *Misguided practice #1: Since people are interested in church, tell them about yours.* This practice advised church leaders to put on dramas and musicals, host leadership conferences, and use direct-communication tools to advertise their special services. The thought was that we could survey our community about their needs, and then meet them. Just get the word out, and people will come.

    While there's nothing wrong with getting the word out about your church, this misguided practice tends to be more effective at attracting Christians from other churches than non-Christians.

- *Misguided practice #2: Since people like to be with others who look, talk, and act like themselves, focus your evangelism.* This encouraged church leaders to reach out to people who look like your congregation because if they see others who look and sound like them in the pews, then they will want to stay, and your church will grow. Behind this strategy is the idea that evangelism is most effective when it doesn't cross racial, linguistic, or class barriers.

  This misguided practice is also known as the infamous "homogenous unit principle," which has been heavily criticized as racist, narrow-minded, exclusive, and antibiblical. And while the originators of this church growth principle certainly believed that the gospel is for all people, they also taught that "homogeneity aids the evangelistic mandate."[3]

- *Misguided practice #3: Since people want their spiritual hunger satisfied, emphasize discipleship.* This taught leaders that people are interested in spiritual matters, so if your programming and preaching are discipling your people, then you won't lose anyone. Instead, you will attract people to your church because of your emphasis on discipleship. The church growth movement taught that "finding sheep running wild in the streets or hungry on the mountainside and bringing them back to the fold is not sheep stealing. It is engaging in Christ's work of finding and folding the lost."[4] In other words, feed people with what they want and aren't getting elsewhere, and they will come in droves.

While you shouldn't turn away newcomers just because they came from another church, neither should you automatically welcome them with no questions asked.

- *Misguided practice #4: Since people want their felt needs met, avoid controversial topics.* Many leaders believe that people experience enough division and controversy in their daily lives, so preaching and teaching should focus on how the Bible addresses felt needs. The idea is that if we show people how the Bible is relevant, they will keep coming back for more.

  While the Bible is relevant and speaks to our every need, don't forget that it also speaks to the areas that your church may not want it to speak to.

Assumption #2: "Of Course, Growth"

The second assumption from the church growth movement that continues to affect church practice today is that growth is the goal. "Lack of church growth is a serious disease, but in most cases it is a curable one"[5] was the mindset behind the movement. In fact, the assumption of growth became such a dominant theme that a shrinking church was seen as a sinning church.

Just consider the assumptions underneath this statement from the book *Ten Steps for Church Growth*: "Church growth is directly related to God's will. God wants his church to grow. . . . Any church not concerned with growth and discipleship is really disobeying

God and is doing what is *not* pleasing to him."[6] Consider also the assumptions behind this claim in the book *Your Church Can Grow*: "It is simply biblical and theological nonsense to argue that God is pleased when churches, year after year and generation after generation, lose members."[7]

While it's true that God wants His church to grow, isn't there a distinct season for everything (Ecclesiastes 3:1-8)? A season to plant, a season to grow, a season to harvest, and a season to rest? And in 1 Corinthians 3, Paul makes it clear that a leader's role is to plant and water, while God is the one responsible for the growth. So to assume that nongrowth is automatically sin is a gross misinterpretation of the Scriptures and an overgeneralization of how God works!

Take, for example, the benefits of a forest fire. While a fire might appear to be a bad thing that must always be prevented at all costs, periodic fires actually help a forest's ecosystem by increasing soil fertility, releasing seeds, aiding seed germination, and destroying invasive species.[8] Much like forest fires, difficult seasons in our lives and ministries often have positive outcomes. This is one of the reasons the Bible encourages us to "consider it a great joy, my brothers and sisters, whenever you experience various trials, because you know that the testing of your faith produces endurance. And let endurance have its full effect, so that you may be mature and complete, lacking nothing" (James 1:2-4). Fire, trials, and seasons of nongrowth have a purpose and shouldn't be avoided or be automatically considered sin.

Here are three misguided ways that this assumption of growth continues to shape church practice today, just as it has been doing for the past several decades:

- *Misguided practice #1: If your church isn't growing, work differently.* Church growth expert C. Peter Wagner suggests five disciplines a pastor must practice to achieve growth: (1) assume responsibility because church growth starts with the pastor, (2) work hard since it's not easy to lead a growing church, (3) learn to delegate because you can't do it alone, (4) be a leader of leaders since you can't pastor everyone, and (5) reject nongrowth theology because God wants the church to grow.[9]

  While these five disciplines might be solid leadership principles, they are not all biblical. And there's a clear absence of *spiritual* disciplines in this list.

- *Misguided practice #2: If your church isn't growing, disciple your church to want it.* Wagner has a parallel list of disciplines that the congregation needs to practice to achieve growth: (1) agree to follow growth-seeking leaders like sheep follow their shepherd, (2) give generously since church growth costs money, (3) invite newcomers into your life and start new small groups, and (4) enlarge the leadership circle by sharing power.[10]

  This is what it looks like to disciple your church to follow your leadership and want growth—but we should actually be discipling people to follow Jesus and want His will, which may or may not be growth at this time.

- *Misguided practice #3: If your church isn't growing, preach differently.* Since we live in an entertainment-filled world, sermons must be entertaining, otherwise "dull and lifeless sermons will send all the guests and many members in different directions."[11] Furthermore, "sermons must be simple, especially those that are designed to reach the largest number. More in-depth preaching and teaching must take place in settings other than the worship service which is designed to reach the unchurched."[12]

One of the reasons that an increasing number of Christians are deconstructing their faith is because they were only fed with simple and shallow preaching.

THE PROBLEM WITH THESE ASSUMPTIONS

Have you seen these two assumptions influence you and your church? Specifically, have you seen them affect strategic planning and decisions that have been made—and that you are now helping make—to reach the lost, disciple your people, and preach the Word? It's unfortunate that some "experts" are still trumpeting the principles that arise out of these assumptions as the only solutions to your church's problems. And as ideas that will help your church grow.

I'm not here to debunk and tear down all the meaningful work and fruit that the church growth movement has produced since the 1950s. And while I didn't go to seminary during the heyday of the movement, my professors did. In fact, I got my master's from the School of World Mission at Fuller Theological Seminary, which was the hub of the church growth movement. On top of that, I'm the lead pastor of a church that has grown in part because of the principles of the church growth movement.

Countless numbers of people are following Jesus because of the fruit of this movement and its later iterations, like the seeker-sensitive movement. Because of these movements, learning effective leadership principles on strategy, change management, recruiting, equipping, and multiplication is now a normal part of the pastoral training process.

However, we would be foolish to expect the same results by simply copying and pasting all the principles from those movements into our context today. Those principles and tactics were written in a world—and to a world—that doesn't exist anymore. The blind spots back then are different from the blind spots today. And although I was able to distill the assumptions of the church growth movement down to two phrases ("of course, church" and "of course, growth"), I wouldn't be able to do that for today's post-pandemic reality because we're *still* working everything out. Things are *still* unfolding, and the future is *still* uncertain. That's why the phrase is "Hindsight is 20/20," not "Foresight is 20/20."

Since context matters, here is how our context has changed and why these two assumptions are problematic today:

- *Not everyone is interested in the church these days.* Pastoral abuse and sex scandals have happened too frequently to be the exception. One too many power-hungry church leaders have looked more like the world than like Jesus. And love of money seems to be as strong inside the church as it is outside it. Because Christians and church leaders are regularly and publicly falling prey to the temptations to be relevant, spectacular, and powerful, people aren't as interested in the church as they used to be.[13] The principles that used to work don't work anymore, because the prevailing assumptions are no longer accurate. We're starting to look too much like the world. No wonder there's been a steady decline in confidence in the church and trust in pastors among Americans since Gallup started measuring this in 1973.[14]

- *We cannot assume growth anymore.* While the global Christian church is growing, the only growth that has recently been happening in the West is the growth of the "nones" and "dones"— those who have no religious affiliation, and those who are done with the church. For the last several decades, evangelism and church growth techniques assumed that people held a shared set of spiritual beliefs—such as belief in an afterlife, moral truth, and consequences to sin, as well as a belief that God (or a higher power) exists. So evangelism and church growth used to be as simple as connecting these "religious dots," as Timothy Keller called them, to prove the truth of the gospel. But with the rise of the "nones" and "dones," a growing number of people believe that the only thing we need salvation from is "the idea that we need salvation."[15]

DISCERNING YOUR PATH FORWARD

Decades ago, the founders of the church growth movement created a compelling case for the relevance of their principles, methods, and tactics, since *what was being done at the time* wasn't working for churches anymore. In fact, they wrote these very words: "Many methods in current use . . . are supposed to bring people to Christ, but they don't. They are supposed to multiply churches, but they don't. They are supposed to improve society, but they don't."[16]

I believe we have reached an impasse once more. The time has come again for us to reevaluate what we've been doing and discern our path forward. It's a discipleship opportunity that we should embrace! So if you want to disciple your people to know Jesus deeply and experience being known by Him fully; if you want to equip your people to reach those they live, work, study, and play with; and if you want to preach effectively in this post-everything world, then start by uncovering your assumptions, studying your context, and trusting the Holy Spirit.

UNCOVER YOUR ASSUMPTIONS

In this chapter, we've unpacked two assumptions that have long undergirded church leadership: the assumption that everyone is still generally interested in the church, and the assumption that each church should always be growing. To make the most of this book, take some time to shoulder-check whether these assumptions are blind spots for you by answering the following questions.

1. Have you seen these assumptions shape the way you evangelize, disciple, and preach? If so, how?

_____

_____

_____

2. Have you seen these assumptions drive the way ministry happens in your church? If so, where?

STUDY YOUR CONTEXT

Do you *know* the people in your church? I'm referring to your church right now, your regulars. I'm not just asking if you know their names or would recognize them at the grocery store. I'm asking if you know their stories, their pain, their joy, and how they came to know Christ. *Do* they know Christ? Did they come to know Christ at your church? Do they want to be known by Christ? Do they want to make Christ known?

I recognize these are difficult questions to answer for churches that are larger than fifty people, but it's important that church leaders try to take the spiritual temperature of their church from time to time. Let the following questions be your spiritual thermometer to gauge where things are at.

1. Think back to the last several people who were baptized at your church. What did their stories tell you about your church?

----

2. What posture do people have when they gather on the weekends at your church? Are they expectant and hungry? Are they there out of obligation and tradition? Or are they somewhere in between?

_____

_____

_____

3. How often are your people inviting and bringing newcomers to your church? What does this tell you about their faith and your church?

_____

_____

_____

TRUST THE HOLY SPIRIT

Have you ever considered whose responsibility it is to awaken the spiritually sleeping and dead into a vibrant relationship with Christ? Or whose responsibility it is to grow the spiritual seeds that you've planted and watered through your preaching, discipleship, and evangelism? While individual disciples and the gathered church have a specific role to play in each of those processes, the ultimate responsibility lies with the Holy Spirit. It is the Spirit who will build the church and make sure that the gates of hell never prevail against her. Perhaps you believe this to be true, but do your actions show it? Answer the following questions to see how your methods and tactics line up with your theology.

1. When you preach, are you trying to stir interest in Jesus? Or are you trying to facilitate an encounter with Jesus?

2. How much time do you spend praying during your sermon preparation process, as you disciple others, and in your evangelism? How does this compare with the total time you spend doing each of these activities?

3. Whom (or what) do you turn to when people leave your church? When your attendance goes down? When giving is behind budget? Or when there's political or social pressure against the church?

TEAM DISCUSSION QUESTIONS

1. Did you resonate with the assumptions related to church growth discussed in this chapter? Discuss how you've seen them in your church or another church that you've been a part of.

2. Are there other assumptions that drive the way ministry happens in your church? If so, what are they? And how do they drive ministry?

3. What did you discover about yourself and your church through answering the questions in the "Study Your Context" and "Trust the Holy Spirit" sections?

A NEW FRAMEWORK
FOR THE NEW OPPORTUNITY

I planted, Apollos watered, but God gave the growth.

So, then, neither the one who plants nor the one who waters

is anything, but only God who gives the growth.

1 CORINTHIANS 3:6-7

IT'S NOT UNCOMMON FOR ME to schedule meetings with members of our church. Sometimes they want to talk about life, and other times we meet to discuss matters of ecclesiology or theology. One of these meetings that I'll never forget was one I had years ago with a longtime member of our church. She wanted to discuss finances and stewardship, but it wasn't this topic that made the conversation so memorable. Rather, it was when she started referring to our church as *"your* church."

This caught me by surprise. *"My* church?" I blurted out. She was not an outsider. She had been a part of our church for decades. So without even thinking that I might offend her, I replied, "Don't you mean *our* church?"

Why did she refer to Beulah as "*your* church"?[1] I may be the lead pastor, but the church is not mine. Was it a result of the way I was talking about Beulah? Was this her subtle way of telling me that she was disengaging from our church, getting ready to leave? Or was this a sign that something bigger was shifting in our culture, and the way that we used to *do* church had to change?

I think of this exchange often when I consider the importance of knowing our congregants, studying our context, and taking the spiritual temperature of our churches. If church leaders aren't taking the time and making the space to observe and think about what's happening around them, they might miss the subtle changes that are taking place.

For example, do you have *margin* in your life, like the white spaces between these words and the edges of the page? Having margin is about intentionally scheduling *white space* in your calendar to pray, rest, read, plan, hear from others, and listen to what's going on around you in order to discern what's next. Is margin a part of your daily and weekly rhythms? Or are you constantly going from one meeting to another—often arriving late? Do you have space to breathe between sermons? Or do you feel like you never have enough time to prepare? And do you know how it feels to be all caught up on your emails? Or are you constantly apologizing for late or missed replies?

When we lack margin, we often miss the subtle changes that are happening all around us. We don't have the space to detect and discern them, let alone respond! We notice big events, like global pandemics, social unrest, local tragedies, government changes, and viral trends (do you remember the tortilla slap challenge?), but it's the subtleties that go unnoticed. Subtle changes like shifting assumptions and changing language in our culture and church.

This is why I schedule margin into my calendar. Not only does it keep me grounded, but having the margin to meet with and listen to people in my church family helps me remember that I am *not* what I do, and that my identity isn't tied to the size of my church, because my worth doesn't come from any of that.[2] So whether it's a formal sit-down over coffee or a meal, or an informal encounter in the neighborhood, grocery store, or church hallway, margin gives me the space to have these conversations and to listen. And it's in these conversations where I often discern the subtle changes that are happening in our culture and church.

In the last chapter, I asked you to spend some time studying your context by discerning who is part of your church and what their posture toward God is. After all, it's important that you, as a church leader, have an idea where your congregants are at spiritually and what the spiritual temperature of your church is. And while I have provided some guidance to help you figure these things out, I'll admit it's not always clear-cut.

Historically, church leaders have used some sort of scale from *non-Christian* to *Christian* to identify where an individual might be spiritually, but there is a problem with this linear framework: It is based on false assumptions that don't account for the reality of our post-everything world.

THE NON-CHRISTIAN TO CHRISTIAN SCALE

One of the foundational principles from the church growth movement was James F. Engel's linear scale that outlined the progressive steps that a person will go through on their journey from non-Christian to Christian. This paradigm was used for a long time as an evangelism framework for churches (Figure 2.1).

THE ENGEL SCALE

-8	Awareness of a supreme being, but no effective knowledge of the gospel
-7	Initial awareness of the gospel
-6	Awareness of the fundamentals of the gospel
-5	Grasp of the implications of the gospel
-4	Positive attitude toward the gospel
-3	Personal problem recognition
-2	Decision to act
-1	Repentance and faith in Christ
The person is regenerated and becomes a new creation in Christ	
+1	Post-decision evaluation

Figure 2.1

As you'll see with the starting point of this scale (awareness of a supreme being), this principle was a product of its time, governed by the assumptions of its day. If Engel were to rewrite the scale today in our post-everything world, I wonder how far back he would go. Perhaps it would start at "hostility and antagonism toward spiritual matters." Or possibly at "no framework for a supreme being."

There have been many variations of this linear paradigm of evangelism. John Wimber's Involvement Axis starts with "pagan pool" at one end and places "active members—strong" at the other end, with various types of "nonmembers" and "inactive members" in the middle. Alan R. Tippett's scale outlines three phases: awareness, decision, and incorporation. And John Wimber and R. Daniel Reeves's scale measures belonging and intimacy.[3]

Essentially, the Engel Scale and all its variations can be simplified with this diagram below (Figure 2.2). On this scale, there are non-Christians and Christians. On the far left are those who are far from God, and on the far right are those who are mature, multiplying disciples of Christ. And in the middle, there is a distinct point and moment of salvation where the person becomes a new creation in Christ.

non-Christian   Christian

Figure 2.2

For the last few decades, we have seen an incredible harvest and growth in the church because the church growth movement reminded us that we must do anything and everything to help people move along this scale from non-Christian to Christian. Some churches were even known to have core values like "We will do anything short of sin to reach people" or "Saved people save people" to emphasize the importance of the great commission. As a result, these churches would often refer to non-Christians as *seekers* and Christians as *disciples*.

THE INTERESTED

As we covered in chapter 1, two foundational assumptions that began in the 1950s continue to affect church practice today. One of them is the assumption "of course, church," which assumes that everyone is generally interested in the church. *If* this were still true, *then* there would be only two types of people in our communities, and both would be interested in spiritual things:

- *Interested non-Christians.* These are the seekers—the non-Christians who are curious about faith, church, and spirituality. They occasionally attend church but have not made a commitment to following Jesus.

- *Interested Christians.* These are the disciples—the Christians who are committed followers of Jesus and consistent churchgoers.

The scale would look something like this:

SEEKER	DISCIPLE
non-Christian	Christian

Figure 2.3

But as we've seen over the last few years, this paradigm no longer holds up! We can't assume that every non-Christian is interested in or curious about the church anymore. And we can't assume that every Christian is interested in the church either. Many people have no interest at all.

THE UNINTERESTED

Now let's talk about the uninterested. As with the interested, there are two subcategories of people uninterested in spiritual matters:

- *Uninterested non-Christians.* These are the sleepers—the people who aren't interested in faith or spirituality or church. Sometimes we see uninterested non-Christians in our churches, though it's rare. If they make it into the building, often they have external motivations, like wanting to appease a parent, meet a significant other, or expand their network. When churches went exclusively online during the pandemic, there was less of a reason for non-Christians to "go to church," especially if they weren't interested in Jesus. Today, many non-Christians haven't returned—and don't see a need to—if they aren't interested in faith or spirituality. Biblically speaking, they are spiritually asleep.

  Sleeping and awakening is a common metaphor in the Scriptures for salvation. When Paul says, "Awake, O sleeper, rise up from the dead, and Christ will give you light" (Ephesians 5:14, NLT), he is explaining that salvation is about waking up from our spiritual slumber. I love how theologian John Stott explains this passage: "Here our former condition in Adam is graphically described in terms of sleep, death and darkness, from all of which Christ rescues us. Conversion is nothing less than awaking out of sleep, rising from death and being brought out of darkness into the light of Christ. No wonder we are summoned to live a new life in consequence!"[4]

- *Uninterested Christians.* These are the consumers—the Christians who "go to church" but are uninterested in becoming disciples. These uninterested Christians are the people who appreciated the pandemic quarantine restrictions because they could stream your service, then their favorite celebrity pastor's service, and then another, and another. But eventually, they realized that no one would notice if they didn't attend in person regularly post-pandemic. After all, they could just watch "your" church service later when it's more convenient, right? The pandemic revealed what has been true for a while—that there's a whole category of Christians who "go to church" but are uninterested in the church. In fact, for them, it doesn't matter if they're streaming your service from the living room or sitting in your pews. They are *watching* the church instead of *being* the church.

THE INTERESTED/UNINTERESTED MATRIX

Just like our communities and churches have people everywhere along the non-Christian to Christian scale, the same is true with the uninterested and the interested—it's also a scale. When you put both scales together, you get the Interested/Uninterested Matrix (Figure 2.4).

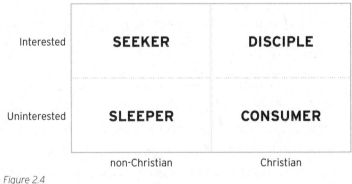

Figure 2.4

In part 2 of this book, we will unpack each quadrant of this matrix in detail—who they are, how to reach them, how to disciple them, and how to speak to them. While it would certainly be nice if there were just *one* way to reach, disciple, and speak to *all* people, there isn't. That's why Jesus talked about different types of soil in His parable of the sower. He knew that the people gathering to hear Him weren't all the same.

> As a large crowd was gathering, and people were coming to Jesus from every town, he said in a parable, "A sower went out to sow his seed. As he sowed, some seed fell along the path; it was trampled on, and the birds of the sky devoured it. Other seed fell on the rock; when it grew up, it withered away, since it lacked moisture. Other seed fell among thorns; the thorns grew up with it and choked it. Still other seed fell on good ground; when it grew up, it produced fruit: a hundred times what was sown." As he said this, he called out, "Let anyone who has ears to hear listen."
> LUKE 8:4-8

Jesus' explanation of this parable highlights the difference between our responsibility and God's.

> "This is the meaning of the parable: The seed is the word of God. The seed along the path are those who have heard and then the devil comes and takes away the word from their hearts, so that they may not believe and be saved. And the seed on the rock are those who,

when they hear, receive the word with joy. Having no root, these believe for a while and fall away in a time of testing. As for the seed that fell among thorns, these are the ones who, when they have heard, go on their way and are choked with worries, riches, and pleasures of life, and produce no mature fruit. But the seed in the good ground—these are the ones who, having heard the word with an honest and good heart, hold on to it and by enduring, produce fruit."

LUKE 8:11-15

Isn't it intriguing how Jesus doesn't then go on to tell His disciples the "secret" to sowing seeds so that they *only* fall on good ground? He doesn't because that's not our responsibility—that's His! Our responsibility is to sow seeds and water them—not to grow them. This is what Paul was referring to in his letter to the Corinthians: "I planted, Apollos watered, but God gave the growth. So, then, neither the one who plants nor the one who waters is anything, but only God who gives the growth" (1 Corinthians 3:6-7).

With that in mind, let's further define each quadrant in this matrix as it relates to the parable of the sower.

- *Sleepers* are spiritually asleep. They're non-Christian and uninterested in both Jesus and the church. They are like the seeds that fell along the path, got trampled on, and then were devoured by birds. At one point in their lives, sleepers might have attended a Christmas Eve or Easter service and heard the gospel, or a friend or neighbor might have talked to them about Jesus, but none of it took root. They are like "those who have heard and then the devil comes and takes away the word from their hearts, so that they may not believe and be saved" (Luke 8:12). For our work to be effective, the Holy Spirit must loosen the soil of their hearts and open their minds to the things of God.

- *Seekers* are beginning to wake up. They haven't yet decided to surrender their lives to Jesus, but they're interested in Jesus and the church. They engage in spiritual conversations with you. They come when you invite them to church—and sometimes on their own. And they occasionally pray. The spiritual seeds that you've planted and watered are beginning to sprout, but we don't yet know what soil they landed on. Seekers could be like the seeds that fell on the path, on the rock, among the thorns, or on good ground.

- *Consumers* are Christian. At some point in their lives, they decided to follow Jesus, but for one reason or another, they're not that interested in Jesus or the church anymore. They are like the seeds that fell on the rock and grew up, but later withered away because they lacked moisture. They are like "those who, when they hear, receive the word with joy. Having no root, these believe for a while and fall away in a time of testing" (Luke 8:13). Alternatively, consumers are like the seeds that fell among the thorns and grew, but got choked by the "worries, riches, and pleasures of life, and produce no mature fruit" (Luke 8:14).

- *Disciples* are also Christian, but unlike consumers, they are actively growing in their relationship with Jesus because they are interested in Jesus and the church. They are like the seeds that fell on good ground and grew up—so much so that they are now producing fruit a hundred times what was sown. They recognize that every disciple is called to be a disciplemaker, so they are intentionally walking with others. They are "the ones who, having heard the word with an honest and good heart, hold on to it and by enduring, produce fruit" (Luke 8:15).

YOUR CHURCH: PRE-PANDEMIC AND TODAY

Do you remember who made up your church before the pandemic? If so, how is it different today? Have you detected any changes? I invite you to take a moment and try to answer the following questions. You might want to ask others on your leadership team the same questions (especially if you weren't at your current church before the pandemic).

1. Approximately what percentage of your church are sleepers, seekers, consumers, and disciples? Estimate the percentages before the pandemic and today.

	Pre-pandemic (%)	Today (%)
Sleepers		
Seekers		
Consumers		
Disciples		

Figure 2.5

2. If you are having trouble answering this question, what do you think is getting in the way?

_____

_____

_____

Those of us whose churches have social media accounts know how easy it is to learn about our followers, at least generally speaking. With the click of a button, we can know who follows us, what they like and don't like, where they are located, and how engaged they are. But as we all know, pastoring a church is *not* like having an Instagram account.

Pastors are shepherds, and as shepherds, we need to know our sheep. Isn't this why Jesus told Peter to shepherd His sheep (John 21:16)? And why Peter then wrote, "Shepherd God's flock among you" (1 Peter 5:2)? We need to know who is in our flock—and where they are spiritually—to lead faithfully in our post-everything world. And the Interested/Uninterested Matrix will help us begin doing just that.

CONVERSATIONS AND REMINDERS

In the Reminders app on my iPhone, I have a list called "Church Names." When I meet a Beulah attendee for the first time at church or at Costco (I'm not kidding—I've often wondered if there might be a way to start a campus there because I'm always bumping into someone from Beulah), I'll often write down their name and something memorable from our conversation. I started doing this years ago to help me remember people's names because I find it so awkward when they know mine but I don't know theirs, especially if we've interacted before. The thing that has surprised me about this simple habit isn't how well it works (and it really does), but how it becomes a marker in time to measure change. Let me give you a few examples to illustrate.

One of my first entries is "Jared and Sandy. Moved from Calgary in Dec 2020."[5] They had moved to Edmonton a few months after I did because of work and family. When I asked them why they were visiting Beulah, they told me it was because it reminded them of the previous large church they had attended. Now at that point in time—after a ten-minute conversation—I didn't know if they were disciples or consumers. I didn't ask them how they were involved in their previous church, nor did I ask if they were planning to come back the next week. It was a simple get-to-know-you conversation.

After meeting Craig and Alicia, giving them a tour of our newly renovated nursery, and sharing Nashville restaurant recommendations for their upcoming trip, I wrote down, "Craig and Alicia. New to Beulah. He's from Louisville. She's from Seattle." Like Jared and Sandy, I didn't know if they were going to come back. In fact, they said they were church shopping.

"John. Met him at Costco. Just started coming back in person."

"Blair. First time to church since grade 7."

"Johnny. Front row stage left. Blue shirt. He loves COVID because it brought him back on track with God."

Jed, Karen, Brian, Lorne, Matt, Lisa, Kris, Lawrence, Valerie, and on and on. I have hundreds of entries like these.

Whenever I open my Reminders app and scroll through these names, it's always a mixed experience. At some names I draw a blank because I never saw those people again—they never got involved in our church. For those ones, I don't remember much about the interaction. Other names make me sad because those people did get involved—and it seemed like they were growing. But then one day, they either disappeared without saying a thing, or they left after saying a lot of things! And then there are the names that warm my heart and bring a smile to my face because of the positive changes I've seen in their lives. Jared and Sandy have become actively involved in the life of our church. Amid uncertainty, Craig and Alicia are trusting God with their all and everything. I dedicated Lawrence and Valerie's son, and Lawrence baptized their daughter. As mixed of an experience I find it to scroll through these names, I love how they help me measure change over time.

When you meet someone for the first time, they could be anywhere on the Interested/Uninterested Matrix—and there's often no way to know for sure at the beginning. But time reveals much. On the one hand, their absence from your church over time can be interpreted as a lack of interest, which means either that they were sleepers or consumers when you first met them or that they've become one of these things. On the other hand, their presence in your church is often a sign of interest, but not necessarily proof that they are Christian—so they're either seekers or disciples.

In the end, we want sleepers to become seekers, and then we want them to make the decision to become disciples of Jesus. We want consumers to become disciples once again. And we want disciples to keep on growing within their quadrant to become disciplemakers. Our spiritual lives aren't static. We're either growing closer to Jesus or drifting away from Him.

You are likely already aware of the subtle ways that non-Christians and Christians have different postures toward Jesus and the church, but perhaps you just didn't have language for it. I hope this chapter has given you a fresh framework for thinking about the people in your church and community. This mindset shift is the first step toward building a great-commission church in a post-everything world.

As we continue examining our current discipleship opportunity, we will review the importance of a discipleship pathway and consider whether your church's pathway is working. Then, we will do a deep dive into each of the four quadrants of the matrix—one chapter per quadrant. In each chapter, we will start by identifying who the sleepers, seekers, consumers, or disciples are in your church and community. You will then be equipped with tools to map out your unique plans to reach them. After that, you will learn how to adjust your pathway to disciple them. To close off each chapter, you will reflect on your preaching to determine what, if anything, needs to change for you to reach the people in that quadrant.

But first, let's talk about your church's discipleship pathway and ensure that it's working.

TEAM DISCUSSION QUESTIONS

1. What are your thoughts on the Interested/Uninterested Matrix? Does this framework make sense given your experience?

2. Do you have a method for keeping track of details about your congregants that helps you know them? What works for you?

3. Have you discerned any changes in your church recently? If so, how would you describe these changes? If not, do you think there are any changes you haven't noticed?

CHAPTER 3

ESTABLISHING YOUR DISCIPLESHIP PATHWAY

So then, just as you have received Christ Jesus as Lord,

continue to walk in him, being rooted and built up in him

and established in the faith, just as you were taught,

and overflowing with gratitude.

COLOSSIANS 2:6-7

"HOW DO YOU DISCIPLE YOUR CHURCH?"

Often when I ask pastors this question, they think I'm asking how they disciple individuals. But that is not what I'm asking. Discipling individuals is different from discipling your church as a whole.

Some pastors have a deep conviction that discipleship happens primarily through preaching. Others think it happens through liturgy and worship. Some see their church's programs, small groups, or Sunday school as their pathway to discipleship. And then there are those who just hope people are getting discipled by whatever new thing the church is offering this year. Where do you land?

Several years ago, I wrote *No Silver Bullets: Five Small Shifts That Will Transform Your Ministry* as a resource to help churches build a discipleship pathway from scratch. In this chapter, I feel the need to touch on this important topic because a discipleship pathway is necessary to successfully reach the sleepers, seekers, consumers, and disciples in your church and community. And if your church doesn't have a discipleship pathway, don't fret! This chapter—along with the rest of this book—will provide you with enough information to get started.[1]

A SYSTEM OF SYSTEMS

I once heard an acronym for the word *systems* that stuck with me because of how much truth it contains. It goes like this:

Systems are processes that help you

Save
Yourself
Serious
Time,
Energy,
Money, and
Stress.

Just imagine if Apple or Google didn't create systems to design new phones, and they started from scratch each time. Or if Ford or Toyota didn't create systems to detect and diagnose problems (like the check engine light and diagnostic scanning tools), and they had to tear apart a vehicle, down to the frame, every time something went wrong. Anytime something can and needs to be repeated, it's worth the effort—in the long run—to create a system to save yourself serious time, energy, money, and stress.

A discipleship pathway is an intentional system of systems within your church meant to develop maturing, multiplying disciples of Christ, regardless of their starting point. It is not simply a set of classes and programs, although those might be a component of your pathway. I have found that every church has discipleship-related systems, but not every church has a discipleship pathway.

For example, if you are intentional about inviting first-time visitors to an event for newcomers, that's a discipleship-related system. Or if you regularly offer the Alpha course to create a space for seekers to have conversations about life, faith, and Jesus, that's a discipleship-related system. Small groups and invitations to serve in ministry areas are also examples of discipleship-related systems. Essentially, any sort of class, model, or program can be seen as a discipleship-related system. However, it's only when all these systems are working together in an interconnected fashion (instead of working in isolation) that you get a discipleship pathway—a system of systems.

Think about gears. Every discipleship-related system in your church is like a gear. Every gear looks different—both in shape and size—and while each gear works and spins by itself (and with other similarly shaped gears), they may or may not work when connected to other types of gears. This is why creating a discipleship pathway isn't as simple as just forcing your gears into each other. Can you imagine trying to connect all the gears in Figure 3.1 to each other? It wouldn't work. They wouldn't fit together. And the gears that used to work would cease to function, since everything would get stuck.

| Newcomers Event | Small Groups | Alpha Course | Serving |

Figure 3.1

A discipleship pathway isn't a random collection of gears that just happen to fit together. A discipleship pathway is a system of systems. More specifically, it's a system of three systems that intentionally fit together and work together in an interconnected fashion. The three systems are your *ongoing steps*, *first steps*, and *next steps*, as shown below in Figure 3.2.

Figure 3.2

You can scale these three systems up or down—depending on your size, context, resources, and needs. For example, there might be fewer gears in smaller churches, and more gears in larger churches. But regardless of your church size, there will still be three *sets* of gears, representing the three *systems* in a discipleship pathway.

When working together, these three systems are your pathway to disciple the sleepers, seekers, consumers, and disciples in your church and community. Let's unpack what each system looks like.

The System of Ongoing Steps

You might wonder why I'm starting with *ongoing steps* and not *first steps*. I did this intentionally, since *ongoing steps* are the central system of every discipleship pathway. You can think of these steps as the spiritual practices that everyone can do and no one ever grows out of. Unlike *first* and *next steps*, which are both short-term, *ongoing steps* are the practices that you live out while growing as a disciple of—and a disciplemaker of—others.

When a person begins attending your church, the *first steps* will connect and welcome them, and the *next steps* will reconnect them or deepen their spiritual life. The goal isn't necessarily to get people into those steps but to get them *through* those steps and into the *ongoing steps*. (I'll get to the system of first steps and the system of next steps a bit later in this chapter.)

Since *ongoing steps* are continuous practices that will form—and continue to form—your people into disciples of Jesus and disciplemakers of others, it's important that you emphasize the right ones.

According to data from a large-scale research project on discipleship that Lifeway Research has conducted multiple times, every successful discipleship pathway includes these four *ongoing steps*:

- attending worship services
- reading the Bible
- serving
- belonging to a community group

These *ongoing steps* are the practices, rhythms, disciplines, or habits that lead to spiritual maturity. In other words, the more often someone does these steps, the more likely they are to score higher in all eight categories of spiritual maturity as outlined in the research (engaging the Bible, obeying God and denying self, serving God and others, sharing Christ, exercising faith, seeking God, building relationships, and living unashamed).[2]

In light of this research, we revamped our discipleship pathway at Beulah a couple of years ago. We refer to these *ongoing steps* as "The Practices" to emphasize that they are the very *practices* that continually form us into disciples of Jesus and disciplemakers of others.

Churches can choose to refer to these practices in different ways, as long as the principle remains. At Beulah, we call them Gathering Together, Growing Together, Giving Together, and Going Together. Here's a brief explanation of each to show you how we've incorporated the research into our pathway and to illustrate how these aren't one-time programs, classes, or events but rather ongoing practices that you live out to grow as a disciple of Jesus and a disciplemaker of others.

- *Gathering Together: We are a church family who gathers regularly (John 1:12; Acts 2:42-47; Hebrews 10:25).* This practice is about gathering regularly with the church for worship in community. Every time we gather together for worship, we are reminded of what God has done for us in history, we see how He is moving among us today, and we get to respond corporately to who He is, what He's done for us, and what He's doing in and among us. In other words, when we gather together for worship, we learn how to faithfully live as the people of God. And when we gather together in community, we get to practice all that we've learned! In community, we get to live out the "one anothers" of Scripture, and we get to form one another as disciples who make disciples.

- *Growing Together: We are followers of Jesus who grow spiritually (John 15:1-8; Romans 12:2; Colossians 2:6-7).* This practice is about taking personal responsibility for feeding ourselves and continually maturing in Christ. Since spiritual growth is not automatic, it requires intentionality and effort to learn the way of Jesus, follow the way of Jesus, and teach others how to do the same. Reading the Bible and practicing the other spiritual disciplines—both on our own and together with others—are foundational to this practice.

- *Giving Together: We are a team that gives wholeheartedly (Proverbs 3:9; Mark 10:45; Ephesians 2:10).* This practice is about stewarding our time, talent, and treasure. When we recognize that we are stewards—and not owners—of all that we are and have, this practice becomes less about giving what is ours and more about returning what's been lent to us. When we serve with our time and talent, and when we give financially from our treasure, we are declaring that our lives are not our own because we are a living sacrifice to the Lord.

- *Going Together: We are multipliers who go intentionally (Matthew 28:18-20; Acts 1:8; 2 Timothy 2:2).* This practice is about joining Jesus in what He is already doing in the world. When we live our lives in response to the great commission, engaging with and loving those we live, work, study, and play with, God will use us to awaken and draw people back to Himself. This means that going together isn't just something that happens overseas on short-term mission trips—it's something that happens in the everyday stuff of life.

Do you see how and why *ongoing steps* must be the central system of your discipleship pathway? Just like you can't graduate from being a disciple, you can't graduate from these *ongoing steps*. These are the practices that all disciples of Jesus and disciplemakers of others must embody and continuously live out. And here's the great news: The more we live these out, the more we will become like Jesus because we will be doing what Jesus did.

The System of First Steps

When you welcome newcomers into your church, or people who *feel* new because they've been gone a long time, your system of first steps acts like the welcome gate into your neighborhood. The purpose is to identify and welcome new (and returning) people into the life of your church to prepare them for their next step. Or, to put it another way, the goal is to get people *through* your *first steps* and into a *next step*, or directly into practicing the *ongoing steps*. Here are the ABCs of *first steps*: **A**ctions, **B**iases, and **C**lasses.

- *Actions.* When a newcomer walks into your church, what actions do you take to identify and welcome them? Have you trained your greeters to know the telltale signs of a newcomer, like looking for signage or arriving early? Do you have a method to capture the contact information for a newcomer, like a physical (and digital) connection card? How about a system to follow up with them using phone, text messages, email, snail mail, house visits, and/or bots?[3] Remember, these are actions that your *church* can do, rather than actions that the newcomer may or may not do.

- *Biases.* What do you want your church culture to feel and look like to newcomers? If you aren't proactive in setting your culture, then the varied biases—positive and negative—of your volunteers and leaders will naturally come out and create a varied experience for each newcomer. A few examples of biases you can promote for your system of first steps are *personal, fun,* and *going the second mile.*

- *Classes.* Decision fatigue is a real thing, so instead of giving your newcomers a plethora of options to choose from, just decide for them. Focus your language and talk to newcomers during your announcements, on your website, in your social media posts, and in your lists of classes, events, or experiences. Funnel all your newcomers into a single class, event, or experience, and call it something straightforward like "Newcomers Class" or "New to [your church name]."

Your system of first steps will depend on the size of your church, the size of your city and its rate of growth, and your church's posture toward newcomers. But regardless of those factors, the important thing is to keep it simple and be intentional about the ABCs.

The System of Next Steps

Since the goal of your discipleship pathway is seeing everyone embody and continuously live out the *ongoing steps*, you need a system to teach your people *how* to live them out. This is why every discipleship pathway must have a separate system of next steps. Your *next steps* are short-term and temporary steps, initiatives, or on-ramps to teach your people how to live out the *ongoing steps* so that they will know Jesus deeply and experience being known by Him fully.

There are three different categories of *next steps*: discover, deepen, and deploy.

- *Discover next steps.* Any short-term class, program, outreach event, or experience designed to help people learn about God, ask life's biggest questions, and discover what it means to have a relationship with Jesus is a *discover next step*. At Beulah, we've been using the Alpha course for years and have seen countless people discover Christ through this experience.

- *Deepen next steps.* The goal of these *next steps* is to deepen someone's relationship with Jesus. This means that you might have short-term or one-off classes, programs, events, or experiences on spiritual practices, finding freedom in Christ, stewardship, evangelism, disciplemaking, and the like. Regardless of the content and format, the focus is helping your people learn how to live out the *ongoing steps.*

- *Deploy next steps.* These *next steps* are designed to empower and deploy your people for service and ministry. Whether you do this through a class or an experience, the goal is to help your people discover their spiritual gifts, strengths, and passion for ministry while simultaneously helping them find a place to serve.

Your system of next steps is designed for everyone in your church. So at any given *discover, deepen,* or *deploy next step,* you might find a different mix of sleepers, seekers, consumers, and/or disciples. This is to be expected, since the point of your next-steps system is to help people discover (and rediscover) Jesus, equip them with tools to deepen their faith, and deploy (and redeploy) them into service and ministry. The important thing is that no one gets stuck in your system of next steps! This is why I find it helpful to think about your system of next steps as cul-de-sacs for your people to drive in and out of rather than dead ends that they might get stuck in.

HOW WILL I KNOW IF IT'S WORKING?

When I teach pastors and church leaders how to develop a discipleship pathway, I always start with a simple exercise that goes like this. Perhaps you can follow along with me here.

In the space below, write down the first three names that come to mind—within the first ten seconds—when I ask the following question. Don't spend too much time thinking about it, and don't write your own name either! Are you ready? Here's the question:

1. Who are the three most spiritually mature people in your church?

_____

_____

Why did you write down those names? Why not others? In those ten seconds, did you create a list of spiritual characteristics, run everyone in your church through that list, and then pick the three individuals who had the most check marks beside their names? Unless you cheated and took more than ten seconds, then your answer should be no (that is, unless you are a genius or an android).

Okay, now look at those three names and prayerfully answer the following questions:

2. What is it about each of those people that makes you believe they are the most spiritually mature people in your church?

_____

_____

_____

3. Were they discipled by someone in your church or as a result of your discipleship pathway? Did the bulk of their spiritual formation happen elsewhere? Or before they joined your church?

_____

_____

_____

When I do this exercise, most pastors and church leaders don't have a problem answering the second question. They often say things like "the presence of the fruit of the Spirit" or something about being FAT—which stands for Faithful, Available, and Teachable. It's the third question that's the wake-up call, since most answer, "Elsewhere or before they joined my church."

If that's how you answered that third question, then you're in the right place and you're on the right track. Using the principles from this chapter, keep on building your church's discipleship pathway as you work through the rest of this book.

If the three most spiritually mature people in your church were discipled by someone in your church or as a result of your discipleship pathway, that's awesome! Congratulations, but you are unfortunately in the minority. The rest of this book will equip you with different tools and a new perspective—in light of this post-everything world that we are living in—to continue the good work of discipleship that you are already doing.

TEAM DISCUSSION QUESTIONS

1. What did you discover when you walked through the exercise in the last section of this chapter?

2. Take some time to do an inventory of all the steps, classes, and processes you have in your church. Do you have *first*, *next*, and *ongoing steps*? If so, categorize them accordingly.

3. In light of what you learned in this chapter, would you say that your church has a clear discipleship pathway? If not, what systems could you change or add so that all the gears are working together as a system of systems meant to develop maturing, multiplying disciples of Christ, regardless of one's starting point?

PART TWO

DISCERNING YOUR
CHURCH'S PATH
FORWARD

Ministering to the

Four Types of People

in Your Congregation

and Community

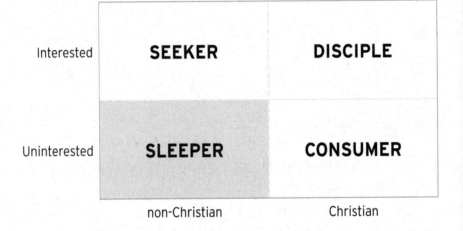

CHAPTER 4

WAKING
THE SLEEPERS

Then he said to me,

"Son of man, can these bones live?"

I replied, "Lord God, only you know."

EZEKIEL 37:3

"I DON'T KNOW IF YOU'RE A MAN OF FAITH OR NOT, but as we were praying about what happened, we sensed God asking us to let it go and extend grace to you in this situation," I wrote.

Darien never emailed me back after that.

Here's the backstory: It was a cold winter day in Edmonton, so I did the gentlemanly thing by picking up my family at the mall entrance instead of having them walk through the snow and ice with me. A large group of young adults was loitering around the entrance. I couldn't have imagined that one of them would shove someone into the side of our car, so I stopped at the entrance and picked up my family. And that's when it happened—that's when Darien dented our minivan by pushing a girl into the side of it.

Eventually, the police came and told me that if I wanted to get my vehicle fixed, I had to talk to the culprit—whom the mall security and the police apparently already knew—to figure things out. So we exchanged contact information, and Darien told me that he would pay to fix our van and make things right, but he would have to pick up more shifts at work to be able to do so.

I was frustrated and angry. *Of course he was going to pay for it and make things right! What in the world was this guy thinking, anyway? And how could he do that to the girl? Was she even okay?*

Initially, I was going to get a quote for the damages the next day and send it to Darien, but a day turned into a week, which then turned into a couple of weeks, and I still hadn't gotten back to him. And that's when Christina, my wife, asked whether we should even make him pay for the dent. "Daniel, the authorities already know who he is . . . and he told us that he has to pick up more shifts at work to pay for the damages. What if he doesn't? What if he can't? What if he does something wrong to try to make this right?"

That's not what I wanted to hear. I wanted him to feel the consequences of his actions. I wanted justice, not forgiveness. He deserved retribution, not grace! But as I began to pray about it, that's when I sensed God ask me whether I *also* wanted to feel the consequences of my actions. And whether I *also* wanted justice or forgiveness applied to me. Retribution or grace?

So that's when I decided to email Darien. I don't know if he just got busy and forgot to respond, if the email is still marked unread in his inbox, or if he simply chalked it up to good luck. My prayer is that by extending forgiveness to him in this situation, I was able to sow spiritual seeds of grace in his life.

WHO ARE THE SLEEPERS?

Six words. Just six words. After being challenged to write a story in only six words, legend has it that *this* was Ernest Hemingway's response—"For sale: baby shoes, never worn." Isn't it profound how much can be packed into a mere six words thoughtfully strung together?

If I could use only six words to describe sleepers' attitudes toward Jesus and the church, here are some ways I would do it:

> "Spiritually asleep. Not Christian. Quite uninterested."
> "Apathetic toward spirituality. Uninterested in Jesus."
> "The church? Not relevant for today."
> "Christmas Eve or Easter? Only times."
> "Unchurched. Never church. No more church."
> "Jesus? Don't care. Not on radar."

Do you know anyone (friends, family, neighbors) with this sort of attitude toward Jesus and the church? Anyone who has placed some*one* or some*thing*—other than King Jesus—on the throne of their lives?

If so, do you believe that God can awaken them out of their spiritual slumber? To new life in Christ? To a vibrant and living relationship with Him as a disciple of—and a disciplemaker for—Jesus?

I'm not referring to those people who used to come to your church pre-pandemic but drifted away and never came back after you went exclusively online.

I'm referring to those people you know who would never step foot in a church or have a spiritual conversation with you. And those people who believe that they're living their best lives and pride themselves on their self-sufficiency. And also that person who was hurt so deeply by the church, or by someone who claimed to be Christian, that they're living with a huge grudge. Do you believe that God can awaken *all these* people out of their spiritual slumber?

This was the same sort of question that God asked Ezekiel when He showed him a vision of dry bones. God was asking Ezekiel whether he had faith in His ability to awaken.

> The hand of the LORD was on me, and he brought me
> out by his Spirit and set me down in the middle of the
> valley; it was full of bones. He led me all around them.
> There were a great many of them on the surface of
> the valley, and they were very dry. Then he said to me,
> "Son of man, can these bones live?"
>
> **EZEKIEL 37:1-3**

What a horrid picture. Just imagine walking through a vast valley filled with dry bones. Bones everywhere—bones on top of bones—bleached-white bones glistening in the sun everywhere you look, all over the surface of the ground. The fact that these bones were "very dry" suggests that they had been out in the elements for a long period of time. And since the bones were spread out on the ground, this means that the corpses hadn't been buried. Over time, birds and other animals had likely eaten the flesh off the bones.[1]

In the midst of this stark picture of death, God asks Ezekiel a straightforward question: "Can these bones live?" As a priest, Ezekiel is likely very familiar with the Scriptures. Ezekiel knows that with God, all things are possible. He knows that God is in control of life and death. And he knows that God is the one who awakens and stirs people to action. So for all these reasons, Ezekiel replies, "Lord GOD, only you know" (Ezekiel 37:3). He understands that if anyone can awaken these dry bones, it's God!

What happens next is breathtaking—or perhaps the more accurate term to use is *breathgiving*—since God awakens these dry bones through His word and His Spirit.

> He said to me, "Prophesy concerning these bones and
> say to them: Dry bones, hear the word of the LORD! This
> is what the Lord GOD says to these bones: I will cause
> breath to enter you, and you will live. I will put tendons
> on you, make flesh grow on you, and cover you with skin.
> I will put breath in you so that you come to life. Then
> you will know that I am the LORD."
> So I prophesied as I had been commanded. While
> I was prophesying, there was a noise, a rattling sound,
> and the bones came together, bone to bone. As I looked,
> tendons appeared on them, flesh grew, and skin covered
> them, but there was no breath in them. He said to me,
> "Prophesy to the breath, prophesy, son of man. Say to it:
> This is what the Lord GOD says: Breath, come from the
> four winds and breathe into these slain so that they may
> live!" So I prophesied as he commanded me; the breath

entered them, and they came to life and stood on their feet, a vast army.

Then he said to me, "Son of man, these bones are the whole house of Israel. Look how they say, 'Our bones are dried up, and our hope has perished; we are cut off.' Therefore, prophesy and say to them, 'This is what the Lord GOD says: I am going to open your graves and bring you up from them, my people, and lead you into the land of Israel. You will know that I am the LORD, my people, when I open your graves and bring you up from them. I will put my Spirit in you, and you will live, and I will settle you in your own land. Then you will know that I am the LORD. I have spoken, and I will do it. This is the declaration of the LORD.'"

EZEKIEL 37:4-14

Just like God created the heavens, the earth, and everything in them through His word, He is re-creating or awakening these dry bones through the power of His word: "'This is what the Lord GOD says to these bones: I will cause breath to enter you, and you will live.' . . . And they came to life and stood on their feet, a vast army" (Ezekiel 37:5, 10). This is the same power that was at work during Creation, when all God had to do was speak, and then things happened! The repeated spoken pattern of "Then God said . . . and it was so" (Genesis 1) is how "the heavens and the earth and everything in them were completed" (Genesis 2:1).

However, it's not just through His word but through His word *and* His Spirit that God created everything and is awakening these dry bones! After all, before God spoke the command "Let there be light," we read in Genesis 1:2 that "the Spirit of God was hovering over the surface of the waters." The word of God and the Spirit of God are inseparable.

In the same way, we see the interaction of God's word *and* Spirit in awakening these dry bones. In Ezekiel 37:10, when "the breath entered [the dry bones], and they came to life and stood on their feet, a vast army," there's no denying that this was a work of God's Spirit. But the fact that the Hebrew word for "breath" in this verse (*rûaḥ*) is the same word translated as "Spirit" in verse 14 makes the connection even clearer that these dry bones were awakened by the word of God *and* the Spirit of God. Just consider the full verse: "I will put my *Spirit* in you, and you will live, and I will settle you in your own land. Then you will know that I am the LORD. *I have spoken*, and I will do it. This is the declaration of the LORD" (Ezekiel 37:14, emphasis mine). Do you see the connection here between God's word and His Spirit?

When God breathed into these dry bones, He was awakening them through His Holy Spirit. He was redeeming these dry bones—redeeming what was lost, redeeming what was asleep, and redeeming what was dead. In the same way, when God awakens the sleepers around you, He will do so through His word and Spirit. But He won't do it alone—not because He can't, but because He wants to do it together with you and me!

Isn't that incredible? While God didn't need Ezekiel to awaken the dry bones—just like He didn't need any help to create the heavens, the earth, and everything in them—He invited Ezekiel to partner with Him. Throughout this passage, we see that God wanted to do this together with Ezekiel because that's who God is, and that's how God works! Just like God invited Ezekiel to partner with Him in awakening those dry bones, He is inviting us to partner with Him to awaken the sleepers around us.

When we say yes to God like Ezekiel did in the valley of dry bones, not only will our faith deepen, but we will also get to experience the excitement of partnering with God and joining Him in His mission. And honestly, there's nothing more meaningful and life-giving—on this side of eternity—than partnering with God to awaken those around you.

PLAN: HOW TO REACH THE SLEEPERS

If you've made it this far, you're probably asking, "*How* do we reach the sleepers?" And while we're going to address that question, it's important to recognize that many people in the church—pastors, church leaders, and congregants—are also asking, "*Should* we reach the sleepers?"

Just consider the results from three recent research projects. In 2019, Barna Group found that nearly half (47 percent) of US Christian millennials believe that it's wrong to share their faith with another person in hopes that they will become Christian.[2] In 2021, the Flourishing Congregations Institute discovered that 46 to 48 percent of Canadian church leaders who work with children and youth also believe that it's wrong.[3] And in 2022, Lifeway Research found that 44 percent of US Christians do not think it is very important to encourage non-Christians to trust Jesus as their Savior.[4]

While I find this deeply disappointing, I'm not surprised, given the post-everything world that we're living in. Everything from the authority of Scripture to the doctrine of sin, the exclusivity of Christ, and the existence of absolute truth seems to be up for grabs—both inside and outside the church—but that's another book for another time. So let's get back to our primary question for this section: What's the plan? *How* do we reach the sleepers?

To reach them, you must start by recognizing that most sleepers are neither in your church nor interested in going to your church. Unlike seekers, sleepers are uninterested in spirituality, Jesus, and all things related to church. (Exceptions might include attending church on special occasions like Christmas Eve, Easter, or another holiday; visiting for a wedding or funeral; or going to church mainly for social reasons or to appease parents.)

Now, just because sleepers aren't regularly in your church doesn't mean that you should give up on your plans to reach them! It's just that reaching sleepers is different from reaching seekers. You can't reach sleepers *directly* through your weekend services, discipleship pathway, programs, or outreach events. To reach sleepers, you need to do it *indirectly* through your disciples.

After all, research shows that while the sleepers in your community may not even think about entering your church, they aren't necessarily anti-Christian. In a fascinating study of two thousand unchurched Americans, Lifeway Research discovered that while 67 percent of unchurched Americans are unlikely to attend church regularly sometime in the future, 79 percent do not mind their Christian friends talking about their faith to them if they really value it.[5]

This is why we need a plan to *indirectly* reach the sleepers in our communities—a plan that involves equipping the disciples in our churches to be the good news and to share the good news of Jesus with the sleepers whom they live, work, study, and play with.

PATHWAY: HOW TO DISCIPLE THE SLEEPERS

The plan to reach the sleepers in your community is *indirect*, through the disciples in your church. In this section we'll address how to equip those disciples in their work.

Look at your system of *next steps* in your discipleship pathway (if you haven't read chapter 3, go back and read it first for context). What sorts of *deepen next steps* do you have in place to equip the disciples in your church to reach the sleepers in their lives?

I'm not referring to apologetics. Sleepers aren't asking if God exists, if Jesus rose from the dead, or if the Bible is trustworthy. Seekers are, but sleepers aren't. And while it's certainly important to equip the disciples in your church to be "ready at any time to give a defense to anyone who asks you for a reason for the hope that is in you"—with gentleness and respect (1 Peter 3:15-16)—a crash course on apologetics won't equip your disciples to reach the sleepers in their lives.

Sleepers aren't interested in spirituality. However, as we saw, research shows that they're not closed to it either, since most of them don't mind when their Christian friends talk to them about their faith.[6] The key word here is *friends*. In the same study, when unchurched Americans were asked how they feel about the faith of their Christian friends, 33 percent of respondents said that they admire it, in contrast to 1 percent who give them a hard time about it and 1 percent who try to change it.[7] Neither of these questions referenced Christians in general; participants were asked specifically about their Christian *friends*!

In other words, the most effective way to reach the sleepers in your community is by helping the disciples in your church learn how to be better friends with everyone they live, work, study, and play with.

The BLESS Way of Life

At my church, we have been using a framework for more than a decade to call and equip everyone in our church to reach those they live, work, study, and play with—not as a tool, but as a way of life. It is called the BLESS framework, and it was developed by Dave and Jon Ferguson of Community Christian Church.[8] The acronym BLESS stands for

Begin with prayer,
Listen,
Eat,
Serve, and
Story.[9]

The framework is effective because it not only simplifies and normalizes evangelism in your church, but it also equips the disciples in your church to be better friends with the sleepers and seekers in their lives.

Let me be clear: This isn't a tool for Christians to use on their non-Christian evangelism "projects." What a horrible way to think about evangelism! Non-Christians aren't projects that we need tools to work on. They are lost children of God who need to experience love from the Father, redemption from the Son, and awakening from the Holy Spirit. This is why we teach BLESS as a way of life, as a way of intentionally relating with everyone we live, work, study, and play with, and as a way of partnering with the Holy Spirit to awaken those around us.

I regularly reference it while preaching—as a normal and natural way to intentionally live our lives on mission. We teach it through our *deepen next steps*: short-term or one-off classes, programs, events, and experiences. And the heart of it is embedded in all four of our core values: to be incredibly welcoming, relentlessly missional, intentionally multiplying, and courageously generous.

When BLESS becomes a part of your culture, you will find that the disciples in your church will increasingly do the following: Begin their day with the simple prayer "Lord, here I am. What do You have for me today? Whom do You have for me today? Speak to me and through me today. I am Yours." Their relationships with the sleepers and seekers in their lives will be stronger because they will be better Listeners, spend time Eating together, and find opportunities to Serve them. As all this happens, they will encounter natural opportunities to share their faith Story—what Jesus means to them—and engage in spiritual conversations with sleepers and seekers.

Doing Evangelism Together

We can't and shouldn't do it alone, though! While frameworks like BLESS will equip the disciples in your church to be better friends with those around them, reaching the sleepers in our lives cannot be seen as a solo endeavor. And while I'm obviously referring to the fact that it's ultimately God who saves a person, I'm also referring to the fact that in today's post-everything world, evangelism is most effective when done in community—when we aren't the only Christians that our non-Christian friends know.

I love how my friend Sam Chan talks about this in his book *How to Talk about Jesus (without Being THAT Guy): Personal Evangelism in a Skeptical World.* He points out that "in many cases, the number one reason our friends aren't Christians is that they don't have any other Christian friends."[10] This is because of what sociologists call *plausibility structures*—with community being the most powerful force in determining belief.[11] "So what we need to do," Chan explains, "is introduce them into a community of Christian friends. How do we do this? By getting our Christian friends to become friends with our non-Christian friends."[12] He calls this "merging our universes"[13]—merging our universe of Christian friends with our universe of non-Christian friends.

This makes a lot of sense. After all, if my family and I are the only Christians that my non-Christian neighbors know, they might dismiss our love, interest, and care as exceptions—or as us just being nice—rather than results of our faith in Jesus. But if my neighbors begin meeting other Christians who are living the same way—and they start noticing that all Christians aren't hypocritical, judgmental, or _____ (whatever other stereotype they have of Christians)—this unbelievable way of Jesus will slowly become believable. And this won't happen through facts, evidence, and data that prove the believability of Christianity for them. No, it will happen because of community—and the countercultural love of Christ shown through and among the people of God. No wonder Jesus said, "By this everyone will know that you are my disciples, if you love one another" (John 13:35)!

Now remember, this section is about equipping the disciples in your church to reach the sleepers in their lives. And since sleepers are uninterested non-Christians, now is not the time to preach and proclaim. With sleepers, the point is to be present, to love them, to be good friends, to pray for them, to BLESS them, and to "merge your universes." As you do this consistently over the long haul, the uninterested non-Christians in your lives—and in the lives of those in your church—may become interested non-Christians, or seekers. And that's when you can begin sharing the good news of Jesus in word, just as you have already been doing so in action.

Rosaria Butterfield calls this approach to evangelism "practicing radically ordinary hospitality." In her book *The Gospel Comes with a House Key: Practicing Radically Ordinary Hospitality in Our Post-Christian World*, she describes it like this:

> Engaging in radically ordinary hospitality means we provide the time necessary to build strong relationships with people who think differently than we do as well as build strong relationships from within the family of God. It means we know that only hypocrites and cowards let their words be stronger than their relationships, making sneaky raids into culture on social media or behaving like moralizing social prigs in the neighborhood. Radically ordinary hospitality shows this skeptical, post-Christian world what authentic Christianity looks like.
>
> Radically ordinary hospitality gives evidence of faith

in Jesus's power to save. It doesn't get dug in over politics or culture or where someone stands on current events. It knows what conversion means, what identity in Christ does, and what repentance creates. It knows that sin is deceptive. To be deceived means to be taken captive by an evil force to do its bidding. It knows that people need to be rescued from their sin, not to be given pep talks about good choice making. It remembers that Jesus rescues people from their sin. Jesus rescued us. Jesus lives and reigns. Radical hospitality shines through those who are no longer enslaved by the sin that once beckoned and bound them, wrapping its allegiance around their throat, even though old sins still know their name and address.[14]

While you can certainly teach the disciples in your church concepts like BLESS and plausibility structures through your *deepen next steps*, you can't stop there. You need to help the disciples in your church live all this out in their *ongoing steps*: the practices that you live out to grow as a disciple of—and a disciplemaker for—Jesus. After all, these aren't theoretical frameworks exclusively reserved for those with the gift of evangelism (Ephesians 4:11). These are practical tools for every disciple in your church, since we are *all* called to "do the work of an evangelist" (2 Timothy 4:5), regardless of our particular spiritual gifts. In other words, start by equipping the disciples in your church with these tools, and then follow up by encouraging them to put them into practice—together with others in their small group or community group—to reach the sleepers in their lives.

PREACHING: HOW TO SPEAK TO THE SLEEPERS

Just as the plan and pathway to reach the sleepers are both *indirect*, so should be your preaching. Instead of trying to stir up interest in the hearts and minds of the uninterested sleepers who may be listening to you preach (but probably aren't), focus on the interested instead!

In the next chapter, we are going to be talking about seekers and ways to preach to *interested* non-Christians, but for this chapter, this section is short and simple. Don't preach to the sleepers— the *uninterested* non-Christians. Stop trying to get them into your services. And even if they're there because someone "forced" them to come, don't worry about what they need to hear. Because while they may be there physically, they aren't there spiritually. It's not their time yet.

Instead, equip the disciples in your church to build friendships with the sleepers in their lives. And since evangelism is most effective when done in community, encourage them to do it together in a radically ordinary way. Pray that God will awaken the sleepers in your community to Himself. Trust the Holy Spirit to awaken their dry bones in His perfect timing and with His perfect methods. And when you preach, focus on the interested, not the uninterested.

THESE BONES *CAN* LIVE

Do you remember how we started this chapter with the story about Darien and then a few six-word stories describing sleepers and their attitude toward Jesus and the church? Well, if I were to summarize everything we've covered in this chapter using only six words, it wouldn't be "Try harder. Preach louder. Convince them." Or "Leave them alone. Not worth it." My six-word story on how to reach sleepers would go something like this: "Indirectly through disciples in community together."

Friends, these bones *can* live! These bleached, dry bones spread out in every direction—everywhere you look—*can* live. God wants to breathe His breath of life into the sleepers like Darien in your community. He wants to awaken them to Himself, and He is going to do it in partnership with you and me—with His disciples.

So just like Ezekiel did, may we say yes to God. May every disciple in your church say yes. May we believe in the power of God's word and Spirit to awaken the spiritually sleeping to Himself. And may we trust in His divine timing and method to do so.

TEAM DISCUSSION QUESTIONS

1. What is a six-word story describing your church and/or what's going on in your church right now? Share it with your team.

2. Who are the sleepers in your life? How are you cultivating friendships with them? And how are you "merging your universes" to include them?

3. Look at your discipleship pathway. In light of this chapter, what is your plan to equip the disciples in your church so they can reach the sleepers in their lives?

	non-Christian	Christian
Interested	**SEEKER**	**DISCIPLE**
Uninterested	**SLEEPER**	**CONSUMER**

CHAPTER 5

WELCOMING THE SEEKERS

Only Jesus Christ by his Holy Spirit

can open blind eyes and deaf ears,

make the lame walk and the dumb speak,

prick the conscience, enlighten the mind,

fire the heart, move the will, give life to the dead,

and rescue slaves from Satanic bondage.

JOHN STOTT, *BETWEEN TWO WORLDS*

ASHLEY DIDN'T WANT TO GO TO CHURCH—she didn't *ever* want to go back. After having previously experienced deep hurt from so-called Christians and the church, she had been avoiding everything related to Christianity for years. In fact, church was the last place she ever thought she'd find herself again. She didn't want to be judged for her choices. She didn't want to be preached at. And she didn't want to be around "fake Christians" putting on a "show."

But recently, things started shifting inside Ashley. To her surprise, she found herself asking questions that she wasn't previously interested in, like *Why do I feel empty?* and *Is there more to life than this?* She wasn't as closed to spirituality and faith as she had been over the last several years. So when her friend invited her to church, Ashley was as surprised as her friend to hear "Sure" come out of her mouth.

When Ashley entered the church and things got started, she wasn't sure what to expect or how she would feel. But then, during worship, something incredible happened. Something she had never experienced before. She felt overwhelmed by love. And she felt an immense burden lift off her! Not understanding what was happening, why it was happening, or who was doing it, Ashley asked her friend what was going on.

With a smile that could not be contained, her friend responded, "It's the Holy Spirit! God is showing you how much He loves you and how He wants to carry your burdens. He is inviting you into relationship with Him."

WHO ARE THE SEEKERS?

Have you ever heard a similar story? Where someone who seemed closed to the things of God became more open and curious? Maybe something happened in their life, and they changed. Do you know someone who never seemed interested in going to church with you, but then one day they said yes? Someone who had always seemed apathetic about spirituality but then started asking you questions about your faith? If so, then you've witnessed the uninterested becoming interested.

These are seekers—the interested non-Christians in the

Interested/Uninterested Matrix. Like sleepers, they are non-Christian. But unlike sleepers, they are interested in religion and spirituality. As outlined in the last chapter, sleepers are asleep—they are uninterested in Jesus and apathetic to spirituality. Seekers, on the other hand, are beginning to wake up—they haven't yet decided whether to surrender their lives to Jesus, but they are starting to seek Him from a distance. They are open to going to church if a friend invites them. Sometimes they might even show up on their own, after checking out the church online. Seekers are curious and are just trying to find answers to the questions of life. They don't mind engaging in spiritual conversations with their friends—in fact, most of them want to[1]—but they don't know whom to talk to, so most seekers start by asking Google.

Just consider the following searches that real people have done. This is from Google's autocomplete feature, which predicts what you were about to write by filling in the rest of your search term, question, or sentence after you start typing.

How do I find my purpose in life?
What is the meaning of life?
Why don't I feel loved?
Is there more to life than money?
Why do I feel lost?
Why do I feel empty after . . .
   . . . a breakup?
   . . . sex?
   . . . finishing a show?
   . . . eating?

. . . hanging out with friends?

. . . achieving a goal?

. . . meditation?

There are seekers—interested non-Christians—all around you asking questions like these. They aren't apathetic. They are curious and know that there is more to life than the daily grind, but they aren't fully convinced that they know what that *more* is. So like the way you test-drive a car, they're test-driving different belief systems to see if they work, how they feel, and what effect each one has on them and those around them.

Do you know anyone asking questions like these among the people you live, work, study, and play with? Do they know that they can talk with you? And would you be ready, willing, and able to have a conversation with them on any of these topics? How about in your church? If people come to your church with questions like these, do you have a welcoming and safe place where they can ask them?

Throughout the Scriptures, there's a theme that goes like this: If you seek God, you will find Him. Regardless of what you've done—or what's been done to you—if you seek God with a humble, genuine, and repentant posture, you will find Him. Just consider the following verses:

> From there, you will search for the LORD your God, and you will find him when you seek him with all your heart and all your soul.
>
> DEUTERONOMY 4:29

As for you, Solomon my son, know the God of your father, and serve him wholeheartedly and with a willing mind, for the LORD searches every heart and understands the intention of every thought. If you seek him, he will be found by you, but if you abandon him, he will reject you forever.

1 CHRONICLES 28:9

The LORD looks down from heaven on the human race
to see if there is one who is wise,
one who seeks God.

PSALM 14:2

This is what Saul was doing. He wasn't persecuting the early church because he hated God; he was doing it because he was seeking God. And in those days, if anyone was seeking God, it was him! Saul checked all the right boxes. He was "circumcised the eighth day; of the nation of Israel, of the tribe of Benjamin, a Hebrew born of Hebrews; regarding the law, a Pharisee; regarding zeal, persecuting the church; regarding the righteousness that is in the law, blameless" (Philippians 3:5-6).

Not only did Saul have an incredible pedigree, but he also studied under Gamaliel (Acts 22:3), which was a big deal. Gamaliel was the grandson of Hillel, the founder of a Pharisaic school whose teachings are still prominent today. And it was while he was seeking God under Gamaliel that he advanced in Judaism beyond many of his peers and became zealous to preserve the Jewish faith as he knew it. And this meant that he had to stop the growth of the early church, and the spreading of Jesus' teachings, at all costs.

This is why Saul went to Damascus. He wanted to honor God by stopping the church and imprisoning Jesus' disciples. He likely thought that if he put an end to this uprising of people following Jesus—whom he saw as a false teacher and heretic—then God would be glorified and more people would seek and find Him. So "he went to the high priest and requested letters from him to the synagogues in Damascus, so that if he found any men or women who belonged to the Way, he might bring them as prisoners to Jerusalem" (Acts 9:1-2). But as he was drawing close to Damascus, he was suddenly blinded by a heavenly light and "heard a voice saying to him, 'Saul, Saul, why are you persecuting me? . . . I am Jesus, the one you are persecuting'" (Acts 9:4-5).

Imagine what must have been going through Saul's heart, soul, and mind. Imagine the shock that he must have felt. He had been convinced that Jesus was a false messiah leading the faithful away from the one true God—but if that were true, then how could Jesus speak to him? Jesus had already died on the cross. He wasn't supposed to be alive! And why couldn't Saul see anymore . . . ?

As a man of faith, Saul recognized that he wasn't hearing the voice of a demon, but the voice of God. This is why he replied, "Who are you, Lord?" (Acts 9:5) rather than "Get behind me, Satan!" To hear God respond with "I am Jesus, the one you are persecuting" (Acts 9:5) must've been mind- and soul-boggling! No wonder Saul went without food and drink for three days.

The Bible is clear: If you seek God, you will find Him. Now, sometimes our souls might be seeking after the one true God while our actions are seeking after a god made in our own image, like fame, food, fortune, or false spirituality. But if we keep on seeking, we will one day find God because He is seeking us. This is why Jesus came! His mission is "to seek and to save the lost" (Luke 19:10). He is the Good Shepherd who will leave the ninety-nine to search for the lost sheep until He finds him or her (Luke 15:3-7). This is how Saul eventually found Jesus, how Ashley (from the beginning of the chapter) found herself back in church, and how so many interested non-Christians in your community are going to find Jesus through you and the disciples in your church. It's because God is seeking us! He is seeking the seekers in your community.

And in His perfect timing, through His perfect methods, and together with His faithful disciples, He will breathe His breath of life into the dry bones all around us. This means that the sleepers and seekers in your community can one day become disciples of Jesus!

Just like "God raised up the Lord," we read in the Scriptures that He "will also raise us up by his power" (1 Corinthians 6:14). By the power of His word and Spirit, God will awaken the sleepers and seekers. "If the Spirit of him who raised Jesus from the dead lives in you, then he who raised Christ from the dead will also bring your mortal bodies to life through his Spirit who lives in you" (Romans 8:11).

I love that the promises of God are perfect, trustworthy, right, enduring, and instructive (Psalm 19:7-11). And how "the word of God is living and effective and sharper than any double-edged sword, penetrating as far as the separation of soul and spirit, joints and marrow. It is able to judge the thoughts and intentions of the heart" (Hebrews 4:12). So when Jesus touched the eyes of the blind, they opened (Matthew 9:27-30). When Jesus said to the dead child, "Get up," the girl got up (Luke 8:53-55). And when Jesus said, "Get up, take your mat, and go home," the paralytic "got up, took the mat, and went out in front of everyone" (Mark 2:1-12).

Just consider how the theologian John Stott summarizes all this: "Only Jesus Christ by his Holy Spirit can open blind eyes and deaf ears, make the lame walk and the dumb speak, prick the conscience, enlighten the mind, fire the heart, move the will, give life to the dead, and rescue slaves from Satanic bondage."[2] So through the power of His word and Spirit, would you pray the Scripture verse below together with me? Would you pray this over everyone in your community who is seeking after God—whether they realize they're seeking after God or not? Over the sleepers and the seekers?

> Awake, O sleeper,
>> rise up from the dead,
>> and Christ will give you light.
> EPHESIANS 5:14, NLT

PLAN: HOW TO REACH THE SEEKERS

Remember, seekers are interested in spirituality. They haven't yet decided whether to surrender their lives to Jesus, but they are interested in Him—among other forms of spirituality and faith. They are spiritually curious since they recognize that there's more to life than the here and now. So how do you reach the seekers in your community and church?

In the Bible, we read that curiosity and interest alone aren't adequate for salvation. They are what precedes it, but to be saved, a seeker must confess and believe. That's why Romans 10:9 says this: "If you confess with your mouth, 'Jesus is Lord,' and believe in your heart that God raised him from the dead, you will be saved."

This is what happened with Saul (also known as Paul). After meeting Jesus on the road to Damascus, he not only believed, but he began proclaiming Jesus as Lord everywhere he went (Acts 9:18-20). So instead of going from city to city persecuting Christians, he went from city to city proclaiming Christ! Apologetics became one of the hallmarks of Paul's ministry: He would travel to a city and start reasoning, explaining, and proving in the synagogue or marketplace to whoever was interested that Jesus is Lord.

Having proof that Christianity is true is foundational for belief, which is why Paul did what he did and why Peter said, "In your hearts regard Christ the Lord as holy, ready at any time to give a defense to anyone who asks you for a reason for the hope that is in you" (1 Peter 3:15). This is also why apologetics has continued to be an ever-present and ever-growing field of research and application over the centuries, from the apostles to Thomas Aquinas to Blaise Pascal to C. S. Lewis to Timothy Keller . . . and on and on. Since faith in Jesus requires belief and confession, seekers need to know how and why Christianity is true, which is the role of apologetics.

Research reveals that evidence for Christianity isn't the only barrier to faith for non-Christians. It's an important one, but not the only one. In 2018, Barna Research discovered that non-Christians in the US would be more interested in Christianity if it had a better reputation, if they saw various churches in their communities working together more, and if they had an eye-opening spiritual experience themselves.[3] And when survey respondents were asked how they would like to explore faith, the top three answers—by a large margin from the rest—were through a casual one-on-one conversation, through a casual conversation within a group, and through a person at church. The bottom two answers were through a tract and through a person on the street.[4]

In 2021, Barna expanded their study to non-Christian Gen-Z teens in the US and Canada. They found that American non-Christian teens would be more interested in Christianity if the Christians they knew were less judgmental of their personal beliefs and lifestyles, more welcoming and hospitable, and more humble and aware of their shortcomings.[5] For Canadian non-Christian teens, the first two answers were the same, with the second two being that they would be more interested if Christianity had better evidence to support it and if they had an eye-opening spiritual experience themselves.[6] When non-Christian teens in the US and Canada were asked which environments they would be open to visiting or participating in to explore faith, their top four responses were an in-person one-on-one conversation with a friend, a digital one-on-one conversation with a friend, an online church service attended alone, and an in-person church service attended with someone else.[7]

Contrary to what pop culture often tries to communicate, research shows that many non-Christians are interested in

Christianity, are willing to talk to others about their beliefs, and will step foot into a church to explore faith. This is why the Interested/Uninterested Matrix is so important to grasp. It shows us that we need to reach, disciple, and speak to seekers *differently* than sleepers.

Seekers are in your church and your community. For the seekers in your community, the principles outlined in chapter 4 apply. You need to *indirectly* reach them through the disciples in your church. But unlike sleepers, seekers are also in your church, so you can reach them *directly* through your weekend services, discipleship pathway, programs, and outreach events.

PATHWAY: HOW TO DISCIPLE THE SEEKERS

For the seekers in your community, go back to chapter 4 and reread the "Pathway" section. The same principles also apply to discipling the disciples in your church to reach seekers: Equip the disciples in your church to be better friends with the non-Christians in their lives. Encourage them to intentionally merge their universes of Christian friends and non-Christian friends. And celebrate all this by sharing the stories of when the disciples in your church practice radically ordinary hospitality toward those they live, work, study, and play with.

Unlike sleepers, seekers are interested in exploring faith, so at some point they will want to know the evidence behind Christianity. They will want to know who Jesus is, why He died, what it means to have faith in Jesus, why we should believe the Bible, what the role of prayer is in a Christ follower's life, and more. Some seekers will go to their Christian friends one-on-one with their questions. Others will bring up the topic casually within a group conversation. Some will stream your church service online, and still others will step foot into your church—for a service, program, or class. However and wherever it happens, seekers will look for answers to their questions about life, faith, and Jesus.

There are two ways you can approach answering seekers' questions through your discipleship pathway. Depending on time and other resources, you may not be able to do both initially, but I strongly encourage you to eventually offer both rather than taking an either/or approach.

Offer a Discover Next Step

The first way to answer seekers' questions is to offer a *discover next step* to help them learn about God, ask life's biggest questions, and discover what it means to have a relationship with Jesus. This can take the form of a short-term class, program, outreach event, or other experience—in person, online, or in a hybrid format. Be creative! The point is to create an open, nonjudgmental, and nonthreatening space where people can ask the questions that they are wrestling with. At Beulah, we've been doing this through the Alpha course for years, and we have seen many seekers find answers to their questions and begin a relationship with Jesus. We've offered the course as a *discover next step* in our physical church buildings, in high schools, in prisons, in restaurants, in homes . . . even in a casino. And while you don't have to use Alpha (there are alternatives), I find their material and training helpful and conducive for seekers to begin engaging with Jesus and the church.

Equip the Disciples to Listen and Respond

The second way to answer seekers' questions is to equip the disciples in your church to answer them! The easiest way to do this is by inviting the disciples in your church to participate with their interested and seeking non-Christian friends in whichever *discover next step* you offer. By listening to the content, hearing the questions that non-Christians are asking, and learning how others respond, the disciples in your church will be better equipped to engage in spiritual conversations with non-Christians. Just ensure that your *discover next step* covers all the major questions that seekers are asking these days: questions about God, life, faith, meaning, evil and suffering, prayer, the Bible, and the church.

Another way to do this is by offering a *deepen next step* on apologetics and/or evangelism for the disciples in your church. You can cover the same topics, but in a classroom environment with a textbook. Now, whatever curriculum you decide on—and in whatever format you decide to offer this *next step*—just make sure that you aren't solely focusing on information transfer. So in addition to teaching about the evidence for Christianity, teach your disciples how to communicate the gospel as a story, how to use different metaphors for gospel presentations, and how to share their testimonies in a winsome way. Give them the opportunity to witness to each other during the class. Assign them homework to practice what they're learning. And pray together—asking God to provide everyone with opportunities to use what they've learned with the non-Christians in their lives.

Books like C. S. Lewis's *Mere Christianity*, Lee Strobel's *The Case for Christ*, Timothy Keller's *The Reason for God*, and Josh and

Sean McDowell's *Evidence That Demands a Verdict* are bestsellers on apologetics. On evangelism, I recommend Sam Chan's *How to Talk about Jesus* and *Evangelism in a Skeptical World*, in addition to Rosaria Butterfield's *The Gospel Comes with a House Key*, Kyle Idleman's *One at a Time*, Dave and Jon Ferguson's *B.L.E.S.S.*, and Jimmy Scroggins and Steve Wright's *Turning Everyday Conversations into Gospel Conversations* as helpful resources to equip your people to evangelize in today's post-everything world.

PREACHING: HOW TO SPEAK TO THE SEEKERS

Because of the influence of the church growth movement and its two foundational assumptions that continue to affect church practice today (see chapter 1), many churches began gearing their worship services toward "seekers"—which meant non-Christians in a general sense. Leading experts in this seeker-friendly style of ministry taught that we need to be attractive by doing *whatever* it takes to get people in the building, like putting on musicals, performing secular music, and sharing felt-need talks, among other tactics. As a result, many church services became so seeker friendly over time that they stopped being worshipful and meaningful for Christians. They became so focused on being friendly and helpful to non-Christians that they became unfriendly and unhelpful to Christians.

In the post-everything world that we're living in, this seeker-friendly style is no longer relevant. Non-Christians won't go to your church because you're putting on a substandard musical, because your "band" is playing a Taylor Swift song as an opener, or because you're giving a TED-style talk. Felt-need talks no longer attract seekers into the church because non-Christians don't think of the church as a center for knowledge and community anymore. And they won't be going to the church for entertainment, either. If they want any of that, they'll just buy tickets to a performance (or watch it on YouTube), stream a docuseries, or listen to a podcast.

You don't need to focus on attracting non-Christians to your church! If they're uninterested, then they're sleeping, and we need to cultivate friendships with them while praying that God would awaken them like He did with the dry bones. If they're interested, then they're seeking, and they will come to your church, so focus on helping them encounter the One their souls are longing for. Help them meet the living God instead of dumbing down your services and preaching.

Just because seekers are interested in God doesn't mean they're automatically interested in everything you have to say, so be interesting, engaging, and passionate in your preaching. Work on your craft by seeking feedback, getting coaching, watching and listening to your past messages, reading books, listening to podcasts, and going to seminars. Prayerfully study the commentaries, but don't preach like you're giving an academic lecture. Preach like you're snatching people from the fires of hell (Jude 1:23), because this is literally a matter of life and death! And preach with a pure heart, full of the Holy Spirit, and wholly surrendered to God because "the most privileged and moving experience a preacher can ever have is when, in the middle of a sermon, a strange hush descends upon the congregation. The sleepers have woken up, the coughers have stopped coughing, and the fidgeters are sitting still. No eyes or minds are wandering. Everybody is attending, though not to the preacher. For the preacher is forgotten, and the people are face to face with the living God, listening to his still, small voice."[8]

This is when the eyes of seekers will be opened. This is when they will meet Jesus like Saul met Jesus on the road to Damascus. Not through entertainment or through an effort to stir up interest in God. But rather when we help them have an encounter with the living God through His word and Spirit. So as Paul said to Timothy:

> Preach the word; be ready in season and out of season; correct, rebuke, and encourage with great patience and teaching. For the time will come when people will not tolerate sound doctrine, but according to their own desires, will multiply teachers for themselves because they have an itch to hear what they want to hear. They will turn away from hearing the truth and will turn aside to myths. But as for you, exercise self-control in everything, endure hardship, do the work of an evangelist, fulfill your ministry.
>
> 2 TIMOTHY 4:2-5

SCREEN DOORS

When we first moved to Edmonton in 2010, we bought a fixer-upper—a small 1958 bungalow on the north side of town with a crab-apple tree in the backyard. Over the years, we began renovating the entire house—from ripping out the carpet and refinishing the original hardwood floors to replacing a load-bearing wall with a beam to putting in a brand-new kitchen to reinsulating and putting vinyl siding over the original stucco and more. We basically did everything to update the home and make it ours—and this was before Chip and Joanna Gaines had their own TV show!

When we finished the exterior renovations, we decided to rip out the ugly screen door and not replace it. We painted our front door jet black and didn't want anything to obstruct it. It was a statement piece.

This was our first home, and like I mentioned above, we had just moved to Edmonton at the time, so we weren't used to living in a climate that would get as cold as -35°C in the winter and as warm as 35°C in the summer (that's -31°F to 95°F, for all my American friends). And we didn't understand why people had screen doors . . . until we didn't have one.

When strangers came to the door, we would just stand at the door and talk—and that's when we realized the purpose behind screen doors in Edmonton. In the winter, the added storm panels help retain the heat, and in the summer the screens keep the bugs out while you are talking at the door!

In much the same way, the seekers in your community are like strangers who have come to the "screen door" of your church. Yes, they're interested, but they're unsure if there will be others like them, if they will be accepted, or if they will find answers to their questions. So instead of going in, many are standing outside, looking in.

A screen door could be your online presence: your website, social media, livestream services, podcast, et cetera. Just like many of us will first check out a restaurant online (by reading its reviews, browsing the menu, and seeing how it looks) before going in person, the same is true with the church. Since seekers feel like strangers to your church, many will start by checking you out online before going in person. Is what they are seeing through your "screen door" welcoming? Can they even see through it? Does your online presence make them want to enter and take their first step? If so, is there someone to invite them in? And if they come in, will they find a welcoming and safe place to ask their questions? Will they meet the living God through your services, preaching, and discipleship pathway? Or will they just find what they can find anywhere else?

Like I mentioned at the beginning of this chapter, seekers are everywhere. People all around us are curious about the questions of life. Some are asking their friends, others are asking Google, and at some point along their spiritual journey, they are going to come to the screen door of your church. When they do, what will their experience be?

TEAM DISCUSSION QUESTIONS

1. When seekers in your city are looking for a church to visit, will they find yours? And if they do, what impression will they get of your church? Take some time to audit your online presence as a church by reviewing your website, social media, Google Maps and Apple Maps listings, and how people are reviewing you on all those platforms. Try searching for "churches in _____ (your city or town)" and see what comes up online.

2. Who are the seekers in your life? How are you personally cultivating friendship with them? And how are you "merging your universes" with them?

3. Consider your discipleship pathway. In light of this chapter, do you have *discover next steps* for seekers? And *deepen next steps* for the disciples in your church? What might you need to change or add to effectively reach the seekers in your church and community?

	non-Christian	Christian
Interested	SEEKER	DISCIPLE
Uninterested	SLEEPER	CONSUMER

CHAPTER 6

CHALLENGING
THE CONSUMERS

The pastors of America have metamorphosed into a company

of shopkeepers, and the shops they keep are churches.

They are preoccupied with shopkeeper's concerns—how to

keep the customers happy, how to lure customers

away from competitors down the street, how to package

the goods so that the customers will lay out more money.

EUGENE PETERSON, *WORKING THE ANGLES*

IN MY MANY YEARS AS A PASTOR, I've been confronted by people who do not approve of my leadership style or my preaching. It comes with the territory. But seminary doesn't prepare you for the blow to the ego that comes with reading your church's reviews online. Who knew that just like restaurants and stores have ratings and reviews, so do churches!

In fact, one former church member left a two-star review on Google because they didn't like my Easter sermon. They took to the internet to proclaim to the world that they won't come back until I'm fired or I leave. Ouch.

Thankfully, not all church reviews are bad. Some of them are good, some are enlightening, and some of them are downright puzzling. Here are some of the reviews that people have left about Beulah:

☆ ☆ ☆ ☆ ☆ "Lovely place, lovely people. Very welcoming."

☆ ☆ ☆ ☆ ☆ "Great experience; love this church. Big and educational, insightful. Coffee cafeteria."

☆ ☆ ☆ ☆ ☆ "We've been attending Beulah for 5 years. We love the kids' programming and the youth group. We also love all the different ways for our whole family to get connected and meet people. The lead pastor always talks about topics that are relevant to our lives and encourages reflection and personal growth."

☆ "I'm very disappointed in the church's policy to not support small groups in allowing them to meet at the church."

☆ ☆ ☆ ☆ ☆ "I came here to shoot some hoops and participate in the AMA paper-shredding event. It's a great service for the community. It's the little things that count."

☆ ☆ ☆ "Attended here for 4+ years. It was a good church overall. It is hard to make connections, though . . . ended up leaving for a smaller church."

☆ ☆ ☆ ☆ "Very good price and good services, nice people."

Wait, what? That last review is an example of one that left me scratching my head. "Very good price" for what? We don't charge admission!

When Christians act like consumers in the church, it shows up in a variety of ways. In addition to leaving online reviews, a congregant might call you up and try to leverage their giving to demand to use your auditorium to record their own personal music album. Some people might accuse you of being lazy right before you get up to preach on Christmas Eve. Oh, and let's not forget the people who email to let you know that if your sermons don't "feed" them, they're going somewhere else!

In our consumeristic culture, ratings and reviews are leverage for customers because of the significant influence that they wield on businesses. They empower the customer through a system that rewards and punishes businesses based on the quality and offering of their goods and services. And since you can also rate and review churches on all these platforms, it's no wonder consumerism feels as strong inside the church as it does outside it. After all, it's everywhere. You can't escape it. Consumerism isn't just in the air that we breathe, *it is* the air that we breathe.

WHO ARE THE CONSUMERS?

It's us. We are all consumers. Our consumeristic society has shaped us into perpetual customers, and we have all been conditioned to expect comfort, convenience, and choice everywhere we go and in everything we do. Without leaving the comfort of our homes, we can purchase anything and have it delivered anywhere we want, from a seemingly unending number of choices. Consumerism has turned us into gods. If we don't get what we want—when we want it—then we just smite that business into oblivion by writing a bad review and buying from another company.

Unfortunately, this mindset has infiltrated the church. In the Interested/Uninterested Matrix, the consumer is the uninterested Christian—the person who attends church and considers themselves a believer but isn't really interested in spiritual growth. They are there to consume a service.

We have all played a part in creating this reality. I consider it one of the unintended consequences of the seeker-sensitive movement, which is the most recent adaptation of the church growth movement. Because churches wanted to make Christianity more palatable to non-Christians, everything—the plans, pathway, and preaching of the church—was geared toward getting non-Christians into the church and introducing them to Jesus. Successful marketing tactics used by businesses to attract new customers and retain current ones were the same as those used inside the church. As a result, conversions, baptisms, life-change stories, and attendance metrics became clear evidence that "the stock" was growing. It kept "shareholders" happy and gave them reason to invest even more. This then led to other churches copying the same model, hoping for the same results. Books, conferences, consulting, and a whole industry ensued, propagating this seeker-sensitive model that helped leaders break the next growth barrier by attracting and retaining customers. As I mentioned in chapter 1, one expert even taught that churches should function like car dealerships—the showroom floor is the weekend service that shows and sells Christianity, with the service department being the programs that keep people coming back.

Now, like I said in chapter 1, I'm not here to tear down all the meaningful work and fruit that the church growth movement (and its various adaptations) has produced since the 1950s. After all, countless people found Christ through seeker-sensitive churches! And I'm deeply thankful for that, since I've experienced the benefits of having been mentored by many of those people. But here's the thing: In these churches, people grew as disciples and disciple-makers *if* they went to the service that was designed for them. *If* they joined a small group and went to classes. *If* they served, gave, and took responsibility to feed themselves and others spiritually. But if they didn't, then Christianity 101 is all they would've learned—because that's all that was ever preached. An unintended consequence of the seeker-sensitive movement is that it produced a whole generation of consumers. It churned out a whole generation of Christians who became so used to being spoon-fed that they never learned how to feed themselves spiritually.

In 1970, A. W. Tozer noticed this trend beginning to take shape because of the influence of the church growth movement. Who would've thought that more than fifty years later, his words would so aptly describe the consumers in our churches today!

Why should believing Christians want everything pre-cooked, pre-digested, sliced and salted, and expect that God must come and help us eat and hold the food to our baby lips while we pound the table and splash—and we think that is Christianity! Brethren, it is not. It is a degenerate bastard breed that has no right to be called Christianity.[1]

And here's Eugene Peterson, from the perspective of a pastor, on the presence and problem of consumerism in our churches today:

> If I receive my primary social identity as a consumer,
> it follows that my primary expectation of the people
> I meet is that I get something from them for which I
> am prepared to pay a price. I buy merchandise from
> the department store, health from the physician, legal
> power from the lawyer. Does it not follow that in this
> kind of society my parishioner will have commercialized
> expectations of me? None of the honored professions has
> escaped commercialization, so why should the pastorate?
> This has produced in our time the opprobrious practice
> of pastors manipulating their so-called flocks on the same
> principles that managers use to run supermarkets.[2]

> The pastors of America have metamorphosed into
> a company of shopkeepers, and the shops they keep
> are churches. They are preoccupied with shopkeeper's
> concerns—how to keep the customers happy, how to lure
> customers away from competitors down the street, how
> to package the goods so that the customers will lay out
> more money.[3]

Remember, consumers are Christian. At some point in their lives, they decided to follow Jesus, but for one reason or another, they're not that interested in Jesus or the church anymore. So when they decide to attend, they usually do so as customers rather than as owners. They're evaluating the programs, the preacher, the sermon, the music, and every aspect of the service (even the coffee line) through their consumeristic lens. And if something doesn't reinforce their narrative of comfort, convenience, and choice, then they'll either complain or just go shopping for another church. After all, for consumers, this is "your church," not "my church" or "our church." For them, pastors are shopkeepers, they are customers, and other churches are just other places they can spend their money for goods and services.

Because consumers are already Christian, no one starts their faith journey as a consumer. When someone decides to follow Jesus and become His disciple, they are doing so as a seeker, because seekers are interested in Jesus but not yet Christian. So, then, why do some disciples grow into disciplemakers while other disciples become consumers?

It's because of drift. This doesn't happen instantaneously. It's slow and gradual, like falling asleep at the wheel. No one plans on driving into a ditch or drifting into oncoming traffic. You didn't set your GPS coordinates there. That was never your intention. It just happened because you were tired. Similarly, the drift into consumerism starts when disciples see the church as something to watch instead of something to be. When they see church as being full of people, not family. When they come to take, not give. When church becomes optional, not central. And when everything in the church becomes transactional instead of sacrificial.

PLAN: HOW TO REACH THE CONSUMERS

In chapter 4, I wrote about God breathing into the dry bones of sleepers and awakening them through His Holy Spirit. Remember how Ezekiel's involvement was a picture of how God is inviting us to partner with Him to awaken the sleepers all around us? Well, it's the same with consumers. And while only the Holy Spirit can shake consumers out of their spiritual rut, He wants to do this through you and me—through disciples and through a change in how we approach discipleship in today's post-everything world. What an incredible discipleship opportunity we have!

Here's the thing: You must stop trying to please the consumers in your church and community. Don't obsess over the online reviews of your church either. It's a lose-lose situation. If you try to please the consumers, you'll end up losing the interested non-Christians (seekers) and the interested Christians (disciples). And *when* you inevitably upset or displease the consumers, they'll just go somewhere else that will cater to their comfort, convenience, and choice. And yes, I recognize that by doing this, you're running the risk of losing big donors. And if you lose them, then how are you going to do ministry? Pay the bills? Keep the doors of the church open? Support your family? Those are all legitimate questions, but God never asked you to please people. I'm thankful that the apostle Paul and members of the early church also wrestled with similar temptations. Just consider Paul's thoughts on people-pleasing:

> Am I now trying to persuade people, or God? Or am I striving to please people? If I were still trying to please people, I would not be a servant of Christ.
> **GALATIANS 1:10**

> Whatever you do, do it from the heart, as something done for the Lord and not for people, knowing that you will receive the reward of an inheritance from the Lord. You serve the Lord Christ.
> **COLOSSIANS 3:23-24**

> Just as we have been approved by God to be entrusted with the gospel, so we speak, not to please people, but rather God, who examines our hearts. For we never used flattering speech, as you know, or had greedy motives—God is our witness—and we didn't seek glory from people, either from you or from others.
> **1 THESSALONIANS 2:4-6**

Jesus commissioned us to "go, therefore, and make disciples of all nations" (Matthew 28:19), not to please people who like to hold the church ransom with their tithes, time, gifts, and Google reviews. He is the one who provides us with our daily bread. This is His church—His bride. And Jesus said that He would build His church, and the gates of hell would not overpower it.

So stop doing whatever you're doing that's feeding a consumer-istic mindset, however unintentional it might be. Stop perpetuat-ing the notion that the church is a dispenser of religious goods and services. Stop competing with other churches in your community. And stop making comfort, convenience, and choice a primary lens for decision making—for you and for your congregation.

When you stop all this nonsense, you will start starving the consumers to a point of decision. They will leave your church and continue their consumeristic ways by finding somewhere else that will accommodate and feed their appetite. Or the Holy Spirit will convict and remind them that following Jesus has *always* been about denying themselves, taking up His cross daily, and following Him (Luke 9:23). And if the latter happens—I've seen it happen—consumers will become disciples again. They will move from being uninterested Christians to being interested once again.

PATHWAY: HOW TO DISCIPLE THE CONSUMERS

In the past, many ministries, programs, and initiatives effectively got people into church and interested in Jesus. As a result, non-Christians became Christians and Christians learned a lot of infor-mation. These methods were great at gathering people together and growing them. Unfortunately, these same ministries, pro-grams, and initiatives weren't as effective at equipping disciples to make disciples.

In chapter 3 I wrote about the *ongoing steps* that are necessary in a discipleship pathway, where Gathering Together, Growing Together, Giving Together, and Going Together are the four practices that we are called to embody to grow as disciples of Jesus and disciplemakers of others. If we think of these practices as exercise, then we need all of them to get a full-body workout. Gathering Together and Growing Together are like working out your upper body—it's where most of us start, and we like seeing progress with defined arms and greater upper-body strength. Giving Together is like working out your core—no one likes doing it, but it helps the whole body with balance, posture, stability, and flexibility. And Going Together is like working out your lower body—if you neglect it, your foundation will be weak, and your body will be out of proportion.

You might be able to get away with an imbalanced workout routine for a short period of time, but if you overfocus on some areas while neglecting others, it'll eventually catch up to you. Muscle imbalance can lead to physical issues, instability, and an increased risk of injury. In the same way, an imbalanced spiritual workout has its own set of consequences. For example, many of the ministries, programs, and initiatives that once got people into church and interested in Jesus are the same ones that helped produce consumeristic Christians. The program became the end rather than a means to the end of being a disciple of—and a disciplemaker for—Jesus. So instead of developing disciples who learned how to work out their whole bodies (and help others do the same), many of these programs overfocused on some areas while neglecting others, unintentionally producing consumers in the process. Consumers who might be great at gathering and growing but don't know why they should give of their time, talent, and treasure in response to the great commission. These are like people who enjoy eating protein ("I want meat and depth") but don't want to do any of the workouts.

So what's the solution? How do we disciple the consumers who are still in our churches today without feeding a consumeristic culture? It's by creating a culture in our churches that will either starve them or sanctify them!

Through your church culture, make consumers uncomfortable by clarifying what it means to be a disciple—a disciple of Jesus isn't a spectator or someone who prayed a prayer but someone who is following Jesus, being continually changed by Jesus, and joining Jesus in what He is doing in the world. Regularly remind everyone in your church that following Jesus isn't a one-hour-per-week commitment but an everyday, all-of-life practice that happens as we intentionally gather, grow, give, and go with others (this is your system of *ongoing steps*). And I'm not just talking about preaching! This is about creating opportunities in your discipleship pathway for people to gather, grow, give, and go together.

Giving and going should be emphasized as much as gathering and growing. Every small group in your church should either have a mission focus or see themselves as a group of missionaries. *Deploy next steps* are a great way to empower and deploy people in your church who aren't regularly giving and going with others. For example, a one-time initiative to clean up the playgrounds in your city or hand out ice-cold water bottles on a hot summer day are great ways to begin reminding the consumers in your church that following Jesus is about giving and going as much as it is about gathering and growing.

Some churches unintentionally create a "two-tier" paradigm that excuses "lightweight faith" and delegates all the responsibility to "serious Christians" or paid professionals. Your church culture can challenge this paradigm by emphasizing that the ground is flat at the foot of the cross and that *everyone* has the same primary calling to love God, love others, and make disciples—regardless of where someone might get their paycheck. An effective way to do this is through sharing stories during your weekend service and on social media—not stories from the pastor but from disciples in your church who are living this out. While consumers might expect pastors to talk about giving and going, their paradigm will be challenged when they hear stories from others in their church—others who are just like them.

Lastly, clarify the impact that consumerism has on all of us, and how we are sometimes better disciples of consumerism than disciples of Jesus, as reflected in this chart (Figure 7.1).

With Consumerism . . .	With Jesus . . .
I am king.	Jesus is King.
I make choices based on my will.	I make choices based on His will.
My comfort and convenience are primary.	His Kingdom and purposes are primary.
My money is mine.	My money is a gift from God, and I am a steward of it.
My time is valuable.	His timing matters most.
The church will meet my needs.	I will meet the church's needs.
Faith is a label.	Faith is central.

Figure 7.1

As you cultivate a culture like this in your church, you will either starve or sanctify the consumers. They will either leave for somewhere else that will feed them the sort of consumeristic Christianity that they want, or they will feel the conviction of the Holy Spirit and repent. In either case, you are not responsible for their decision. You are responsible to teach them the truth, to show them how to follow Jesus faithfully, and to point out where they might be better disciples of consumerism than of Jesus, but you are not responsible for their decision and the consequences of their decision. There's a big difference between being *responsible for* and being *responsible to* the people in your church, and we need to be mindful of that distinction. After all, we are prophets, not saviors. We are leaders, not enablers. We are stewards, not owners. And we are to be disciples, not consumers.

PREACHING: HOW TO SPEAK TO THE CONSUMERS

In chapter 4, the preaching section for sleepers (uninterested non-Christians) was short and sweet. The point was simple: Focus on the interested. Don't worry about preaching to the uninterested non-Christians because they aren't there anymore. They've left.

Can the same be said about consumers? Should we stop trying to appease them since they are uninterested anyway?

No! As I've been wrestling with this question for quite some time, I've concluded that we can't ignore the consumers. We need to pray that God would stir and sanctify them, but we can't simply pass over them in our preaching. We can't assume that they aren't there, because they are! They are sitting in our sanctuaries. They are listening to our sermons. And too often, they are the ones who send us "constructive feedback" because they want to "help." So how are we to speak to them?

To answer that question, we first need to recognize that consumers just want their ears tickled. Culture has conditioned them that way, and the echo chambers of social media and the news cycle haven't helped either.[4] Consumers have an itch to hear what they want to hear, and if they don't get it, they'll either complain or go somewhere else. So instead of acquiescing to their demands, being held hostage to their criticism, or being surprised by any of this, we need to

> preach the word; be ready in season and out of season; correct, rebuke, and encourage with great patience and teaching. For the time will come when people will not tolerate sound doctrine, but according to their own desires, will multiply teachers for themselves because they have an itch to hear what they want to hear. They will turn away from hearing the truth and will turn aside to myths. But as for you, exercise self-control in everything, endure hardship, do the work of an evangelist, fulfill your ministry.
>
> 2 TIMOTHY 4:2-5

I love how Chad Walsh, the English professor, poet, and writer whom many referred to as the American C. S. Lewis, describes preaching: "The true function of a preacher is to disturb the comfortable and to comfort the disturbed."[5] And while he wasn't talking specifically about consumers, I believe that this is exactly how we need to speak to them. This is exactly how we need to preach the Word in this season and fulfill our ministry.

We need to preach in a way that disturbs their comfortable lives, disrupts their obsession with convenience, and challenges their choices. To do this, we need to discern what aches they are trying to satisfy through counterfeit gods. What are the cultural and spiritual strongholds that they are bowing down to? Is it money, sex, or power? Is it one of the seven deadly sins (pride, envy, wrath, gluttony, lust, sloth, or greed)? Or perhaps it's one of these nine "cathedrals"—each with their own sacred texts and canonical traditions—that author and theologian Leonard Sweet wrote about in his book *Rings of Fire*:

Blue-Dome Cathedrals: The worship of Gaia, or Mother Earth. One of the "high and holy days that dare not be desecrated" is "the opening of deer-hunting season."

The Cathedral Market: The worship of Wall Street. "Money is god. Economy is religion. Understanding the market is theology."

The Cathedral Mall: The worship of consumerism. "Consumer culture rips off our wallets as it rips apart our souls."

Cathedral of Sports: The worship of sports. "For most of the planet, FIFA World Cup is world communion."

Cathedrals of Experience: The worship of experience. "The sacralization of experiences exists everywhere from food to tourism to worship itself."

The Cathedral Celeb: The worship of celebrities. "A celebrity culture worships the golden calf of personality and cares little for personhood."

The Corporate Cathedral: The worship of corporations. "Steve Jobs dubbed the iPhone 'the Jesus phone' and was quite aware of his status as a tech messiah."

The Cathedral Kitchen: The worship of food. "Food is now a sacred experience, with high priests ('celebrity chefs'), denominations, rituals, and sanctuary kitchens."

The Cathedral of Self: The worship of self. "'Selfies' are appropriately named."[6]

To disturb, disrupt, and challenge the consumers in your church, spend time prayerfully discerning which of these cultural or spiritual strongholds you can dismantle in light of the scriptural text you are going to be preaching through. These aren't the main points of your sermon or the only things you'll be talking about. Instead, think of these as tools that will help you connect and relate with consumers in your introduction, illustrations, and/or conclusion. For example, if the central text for your sermon is Philippians 1:18-26, the pertinent ache consumers in your church are trying to satisfy through counterfeit gods could be the fear of death, or a reticence to think about it. With Philippians 2:1-4, the stronghold you address could be how divisive our culture has become and how that's seeped into the church. With Ephesians 6:10-13, it could be how Christians have often either overemphasized or underemphasized the spiritual world. Or with Mark 1:1-8, you could talk about commitment phobia.

By naming and addressing the cultural or spiritual stronghold that you are trying to dismantle, your sermons will make consumers feel uncomfortable, since you are disturbing, disrupting, and challenging them. This is a good thing because it will move them to action. They will either starve or be sanctified. But it's important not to stop there, or only focus on that. Remember, as Walsh articulated, preaching isn't just about disturbing the comfortable; it's also about comforting the disturbed. So yes, the consumers in your church should be confronted with their sins and idols—they desperately need to be—but they should also be invited into the forgiveness, grace, and love of Jesus. After all, isn't the gospel of Jesus a message of wrath *and* love? Judgment *and* salvation? Death *and* resurrection? Hell *and* heaven? Repentance *and* forgiveness? Salvation *and* sanctification? Trials *and* joy? Restraint *and* freedom?

I'M LEAVING

"I've been trying to figure out why so many of my friends don't like your preaching."

Imagine hearing that come out of the mouth of one of your elders. When he said those words, we were sitting down for lunch and had just finished processing the news that one of our pastors had resigned.

Did the news trigger some sort of subconscious alarm for him? *Uh oh, now we're in trouble. If you're the only preacher, then we're doomed . . .* Maybe this was his passive-aggressive way of bringing up my preaching to tell me all the ways that I was doing it wrong. Or perhaps this was his vote of no confidence, his way of telling me that he was going to leave the church.

So I nervously responded, "What do you mean . . . ?"

"Oh, don't get me wrong. I like your preaching! I've just been trying to wrap my mind around why my friends don't, and I think I've finally figured it out," he said.

Phew. It wasn't what I'd thought.

He continued, "It's because you challenge us. Your sermons aren't just information. You make us look at our lives. You ask us questions that we're forced to answer."

Without even thinking, I blurted out, "Good! If I didn't do that, you should fire me. If all I was doing was just tickling people's ears and never challenging us as a church family to know Jesus deeply and experience being known by Him fully, then I'd be the first one to leave!"

That conversation from a couple of years ago was a turning point for me. It helped form this chapter and our church's approach to consumers, in contrast with our approach to sleepers, seekers, and disciples. The point of this chapter isn't to scorn the consumers in our churches and communities. We need to love and pray for them. The best way to do that isn't by accommodating their comfort, convenience, choices, and criticism, but by challenging them. Challenging their discipleship to Jesus, their understanding of the church, their role in the church and the Kingdom, and who and what they are prioritizing in their lives.

If you implement the suggestions in this chapter, some consumers will leave, and they will likely write negative reviews of you and your church. But remember, there are some things that you are *responsible for* and other things that you are *responsible to*. You are responsible to teach consumers the truth and show them how to follow Jesus faithfully, but you aren't responsible for their decisions.

So lead faithfully and confidently, and when you hear people say that they're leaving your church because your preaching is too challenging (which has happened to me), don't give yourself credit. Give glory to God, who is speaking to and through you to disturb, disrupt, and challenge the consumers in your church.

TEAM DISCUSSION QUESTIONS

1. How do you see consumerism affecting your faith and your leadership?

2. Who are the consumers in your church? What sort of influence do they have?

3. How might you be perpetuating a culture of consumerism in your church, however unintentionally?

4. Review your discipleship pathway. In light of this chapter, what changes do you need to make to challenge the consumers in your church?

	non-Christian	Christian
Interested	SEEKER	DISCIPLE
Uninterested	SLEEPER	CONSUMER

CHAPTER 7

EQUIPPING
THE DISCIPLES

"Who are you, Lord?"

SAUL, ACTS 9:5

"Here I am, Lord."

ANANIAS, ACTS 9:10

"ARE YOU SURE YOU WANT TO SURRENDER your green cards?" the US border agent asked. Then, leaning in closely, he whispered, "People kill for these . . ."

A year after we got our green cards, we gave them back. It's not that we hated living in Nashville—quite the opposite. We loved our neighborhood, church, friends, and work (and the food). And boy, was the process to get our green cards ever complicated, time-consuming, and expensive!

The reason we gave them back was that God said to. Like Elisha, who slaughtered his oxen and cooked them using his plow as firewood after Elijah called him to follow and succeed him (1 Kings 19:19-21), we symbolically cut ties to move forward into our future. In response to my being called as the lead pastor of Beulah Alliance Church, we sacrificed our means of earning a living in the US to move back to Canada.

Now don't get me wrong, we love Canada and we love our church, but from a worldly perspective, the move simply didn't make sense. Our whole family had *just* received our green cards and could now move anywhere in the country we wanted. Numerous ministry opportunities were coming our way—even one from Hawaii—and if we surrendered these green cards, we would likely never be eligible for them again. So why would we limit our possibilities instead of expanding them?

We did it because early on in my discipleship, I learned that being a disciple of Jesus means having the faith, courage, and discipline to live a "Here I am, Lord" sort of life, responding like Ananias when he heard the Lord call his name (Acts 9:10).

WHO ARE THE DISCIPLES?

Disciples are the people we've defined as interested Christians in the Interested/Uninterested Matrix. Disciples aren't passive Christians or uninterested in Jesus and the church, like consumers. Rather, disciples like Ananias are actively growing in their relationship with Jesus. Following Jesus isn't just a peripheral thing that disciples do, in addition to everything else. It's *central* to everything they do. It shapes and informs all of life. Jesus' mission is their mission, and Jesus' ways are their ways.

Disciples like Ananias know that there is no life, meaning, or purpose apart from Jesus, their source of life. After all, He is the

Vine, and they are the branches (John 15:5). This is why at Beulah, we define a disciple of Jesus as someone who is following Jesus, being continually changed by Jesus, and joining Jesus in what He is doing in the world—together with others. We wanted to craft a definition that exuded intentionality, interest, ongoing movement, and a sense of abiding in Jesus.

The Ananias I am referring to is the disciple who prayed for Saul after he was blinded on the road to Damascus. As you read about this Ananias, try placing yourself in his shoes, and reflect on how you might have acted in his situation.

> Now Saul was still breathing threats and murder against
> the disciples of the Lord. He went to the high priest
> and requested letters from him to the synagogues in
> Damascus, so that if he found any men or women who
> belonged to the Way, he might bring them as prisoners
> to Jerusalem. As he traveled and was nearing Damascus,
> a light from heaven suddenly flashed around him. Falling
> to the ground, he heard a voice saying to him, "Saul,
> Saul, why are you persecuting me?"
>
> "Who are you, Lord?" Saul said.
>
> "I am Jesus, the one you are persecuting," he replied.
> "But get up and go into the city, and you will be told
> what you must do."
>
> The men who were traveling with him stood
> speechless, hearing the sound but seeing no one. Saul got
> up from the ground, and though his eyes were open, he
> could see nothing. So they took him by the hand and led

him into Damascus. He was unable to see for three days and did not eat or drink.

There was a disciple in Damascus named Ananias, and the Lord said to him in a vision, "Ananias."

"Here I am, Lord," he replied.

"Get up and go to the street called Straight," the Lord said to him, "to the house of Judas, and ask for a man from Tarsus named Saul, since he is praying there. In a vision he has seen a man named Ananias coming in and placing his hands on him so that he may regain his sight."

"Lord," Ananias answered, "I have heard from many people about this man, how much harm he has done to your saints in Jerusalem. And he has authority here from the chief priests to arrest all who call on your name."

But the Lord said to him, "Go, for this man is my chosen instrument to take my name to Gentiles, kings, and Israelites. I will show him how much he must suffer for my name."

Ananias went and entered the house. He placed his hands on him and said, "Brother Saul, the Lord Jesus, who appeared to you on the road you were traveling, has sent me so that you may regain your sight and be filled with the Holy Spirit."

At once something like scales fell from his eyes, and he regained his sight. Then he got up and was

baptized. And after taking some food, he regained
his strength.

Saul was with the disciples in Damascus for some time.
ACTS 9:1-19

Most times when I read this story, I zoom in on the miraculous
awakening of Saul, like we did in chapter 5. After all, isn't the
storyline incredible? The risen and resurrected Jesus intervenes
and turns His leading opponent into His greatest ally! From
Pharisee to prophet. From challenger to advocate. From darkness
to light, *literally*!

But have you ever wondered why Jesus also appeared to
Ananias? Why didn't Jesus just do it all by Himself? Was He able
only to blind Saul, not to open his eyes? And why did He choose
Ananias and not Barnabas, Mary, Peter, or any one of His apostles?
Did He *specifically* need Ananias? Was Ananias an optometrist or
something?

While we can obviously speculate about Ananias and why Jesus
might have tapped him for this situation, there are only a few
descriptive details that we know about him from the Scriptures.
Everything else we know about him comes from his interactions
with Jesus and Saul. These details are recorded in Acts 9:10 ("There
was a disciple in Damascus named Ananias") and Acts 22:12 ("a
devout man according to the law, who had a good reputation with
all the Jews living there"). Ananias was a devout disciple of Jesus
who had a good reputation with the Jews living in Damascus.

That's why Jesus called on him! It's not because he was an optometrist. It's not because he had the gift of healing (there's no way for us to know that). And it's not because he was a pastor, missionary, scholar, or apostle or had other credentials that qualified him for such an incredible, historic opportunity (we don't know much about the guy). Jesus called on this Ananias because he was a disciple and he lived in the place where Saul was going.

Consider the magnitude of that: Through the hands and words of Ananias, a regular, ordinary disciple, Saul was filled with the Holy Spirit and was commissioned as a missionary. Because Ananias was available, God used him to heal Saul's eyesight. Since Ananias lived in Damascus, he was the first disciple to welcome Saul as a brother in Christ. And as a result, Ananias experienced the blessing of baptizing Saul,[1] who went on to help lead the early church and write nearly half the New Testament! All *that* through a regular, ordinary disciple.

Now, if Jesus did so much through a regular, ordinary disciple back then, and the result was that the gospel was shared with the Gentiles and nearly half the New Testament was written, don't you think He might use a similar strategy today: looking for regular, ordinary disciples who are living a "Here I am, Lord" sort of life? Just imagine if your church focused on discipling interested Christians into regular, ordinary disciples like Ananias who understood that their mission field was the community that they lived in! Imagine how many Sauls would become Pauls, and picture the exponential effect that would have in your neighborhood, town, city, state, province, country, and continent—and in our world.

PLAN: HOW TO REACH THE DISCIPLES

There are disciples in your church and community who are ready to live the "Here I am, Lord" sort of life like Ananias. They are interested in Jesus. They want to grow. They want to make an impact. They recognize that apart from Christ, they are nothing. And they aren't just concerned with being fed spiritually, since they want to learn how to feed themselves *and* others. They want to become disciplemakers. How do you reach disciples like these?

It all comes down to the paradigm shift that I outlined in chapter 2. This is not about becoming a church that "goes deep" and focuses only on Christians while unintentionally building a wall that keeps non-Christians out; a church where the sermons sound like seminary lectures and non-Christians feel uncomfortably out of place. That's the old paradigm. Instead, to reach disciples who are ready to live the "Here I am, Lord" sort of life like Ananias, you need to focus on equipping them.

Equip the disciples in your church to practice radically ordinary hospitality with everyone they live, work, study, and play with. Equip them with the BLESS framework so they can be better friends with the sleepers and seekers in their lives (see chapter 4). Equip them with the necessary training so they can answer the questions that the seekers in their lives are asking. Instead of Sunday morning being the only place where a gospel presentation and invitation happens, equip your disciples with different ways to share the gospel. And equip your disciples to lead the *discover next step* in your church and in their neighborhoods so that they are the ones helping seekers learn about God and discover what it means to have a relationship with Jesus (see chapter 5).

In other words, instead of trying to attract disciples to your church—which the Bible doesn't talk about—focus on doing what the Bible says, which is to "equip the saints for the work of ministry" (Ephesians 4:12). When you equip the disciples in your church for the work of ministry, the spiritually sleeping and dead will be awakened, the church will be built up, there will be greater unity, and people will grow from spiritual infancy toward spiritual maturity.

If you do all this, some people will leave and others will come. The ones that will leave are the uninterested—primarily the uninterested Christians (consumers) since the uninterested non-Christians (sleepers) have already left. As we unpacked in the previous chapter, this is because consumers don't like to be challenged. They want comfort, convenience, and choice. They want the church to feed them, not equip them. And they want the paid clergy and dedicated volunteers to do the work of ministry, not them.

Don't worry, though. As the uninterested leave, the interested will come—both interested non-Christians (seekers) and interested Christians (disciples). And yes, that means you will pick up disciples from other churches, but I wouldn't think of this as "sheep stealing" as long as your focus and efforts are on equipping rather than attracting. It's likely that they weren't being equipped at their previous churches and have found a place at your church where they can grow, make an impact, become disciplemakers, and learn how to live the "Here I am, Lord" sort of life like Ananias. This is to be celebrated because it's a Kingdom win. After all, the more disciples who are equipped to be disciplemakers, the more disciples we will have in the Kingdom, since we will have more harvesters at work (Matthew 9:38).

PATHWAY: HOW TO DISCIPLE THE DISCIPLES

If equipping is the way to *reach* disciples who want to live the "Here I am, Lord" sort of life like Ananias, then how do we *disciple* them to become the sort of disciple that Ananias was? It's the same answer: Just keep equipping them!

Before we unpack a few different ways to do this through your discipleship pathway, let's spend a bit of time exploring how Ananias lived and grew as a disciple of Jesus, since this will inform the content of your discipleship pathway. Like I mentioned earlier, the Scriptures give us only a few details about Ananias. But when you examine the way he interacts with Jesus in Acts 9, you can glean quite a bit about his discipleship from the implicit details in the text. For example, here are four ways Ananias lived and grew as a disciple of Jesus:

- *He spent time with Jesus.* When Jesus called out to Ananias, he didn't ask, "Who are you, Lord?" like Saul. He said, "Here I am, Lord"! This means that he knew Jesus. He recognized the voice of Jesus. And he could distinguish the voice of Jesus from the voice of the enemy, the voice of his past, his own voice, and the voices of his parents and other influential individuals in his life. Now, we don't know how long Ananias had been a disciple or whether he had known Jesus before He was crucified. But when you see the way he responded to

Jesus, you know those details aren't relevant. Ananias knew Jesus and could recognize His voice, which means that he regularly spent time with Jesus.

- *He trusted Jesus.* When Jesus spoke to Ananias, he didn't respond with "What's up?" or "What are you thinking?" so he could hear the commission first and then decide his answer later. No, without even knowing what Jesus was going to say or what He might ask him to do, Ananias responded, "Here I am, Lord." That's trust. And because he trusted Jesus, Ananias started with a yes.

- *He prayed to Jesus.* After Jesus told Ananias what to do, Ananias had a conversation with Him. I don't read this as him backing out of his "Here I am, Lord" trust in Jesus. I see this as a genuine conversation. And isn't that what prayer is? A heartfelt, open, and honest conversation between us and God?

- *He took risks for Jesus.* When Ananias not only entered the house that Saul was in but also placed his hands on him, he was taking a huge risk. After all, although Ananias had received instructions to do this, that didn't mean it was going to be easy. It's one thing to say yes to God in the privacy of your own home, and it's a whole other thing to go to someone who has the power to imprison you and ruin your life. Remember—Saul was on official business to persecute and destroy the church! He had permission to enter house after house and drag men and women off to prison. The only thing Ananias knew of Saul was how much harm he had done to the saints in Jerusalem. As Ananias was going from his place to where Saul was staying, do you think he doubted whether he had heard from God? Do you think Ananias was leaving behind what was comfortable? Do you think Ananias was leaving behind certainty by saying yes to uncertainty? Do you think Ananias was taking a risk here? Yes, yes, yes, and yes! Ananias was exposing himself to danger by going to Saul. Yet despite all these risks, he said, "Here I am, Lord" because his confidence wasn't in his circumstances but in Jesus.

To disciple the disciples in your church to become the sort of disciple that Ananias was, consider equipping them through your discipleship pathway to do what Ananias did:

- spend time with Jesus
- trust Jesus
- pray to Jesus
- take risks for Jesus

While this certainly isn't an exhaustive list or a comprehensive path for spiritual maturity, it is a good starting point. For example, you could offer a *deepen next step* on discerning God's voice, equipping disciples to hear His voice and differentiate it from other voices. You could also offer a *deepen next step* on prayer and other spiritual practices to equip disciples with different ways to cultivate their relationship with God. A *deepen next step* on the power of place and how to live in exile based on Jeremiah 29:4-7 will equip disciples to see their community as a mission field. A *deploy next step* like serving in a homeless shelter, prayer walking in the red-light district, or going on a short-term mission trip will equip disciples to trust Jesus and take risks for Him. And as mentioned previously, equipping disciples to lead a *discover next step* like Alpha in your church or their community prepares them for faith-stretching experiences that will cause them to actively rely on the Holy Spirit, like Ananias.

Be prayerfully creative with the different types of *next steps* that you offer to equip the disciples in your church and how you offer them. They don't have to happen in a classroom in your church—after all, Jesus discipled His followers as they were going from one place to the next—nor do they need to be taught by a pastor. And use principles of adult education, like flipping the classroom and the 70:20:10 principle (I wrote about both at length in my book *No Silver Bullets: Five Small Shifts That Will Transform Your Ministry*). Ultimately, the point is to equip disciples so they can then equip other disciples, who can then equip other disciples, and on and on. I love how Paul puts it in 2 Timothy 2:2: "Pass on what you heard from me—the whole congregation saying Amen!—to reliable leaders who are competent to teach others" (MSG).

Think about your system of next steps like training wheels. They're helpful in learning how to ride a bike, but you don't want to be a thirty-year-old still using them! In other words, all your *discover, deepen,* and *deploy next steps* should be designed as short-term and temporary steps, classes, programs, events, or experiences to equip your disciples to live out the *ongoing steps* so that they will know Jesus deeply and experience being known by Him fully. So that they will grow into "Here I am, Lord" sorts of disciples like Ananias who see their community as their mission field. And so that they will grow as disciples of—and disciplemakers for—Jesus.

PREACHING: HOW TO SPEAK TO THE DISCIPLES

If equipping is how we *reach* and *disciple* disciples, then how do you think we are to *speak* to them? How do we preach in such a way that the disciples in our churches will grow as disciples of Jesus and disciplemakers of others? It's the same answer once again: by equipping them!

I have found that most of the Christians in my church think the primary purpose of preaching is to feed the congregation. In fact, in the past I've had many Christians—both disciples and consumers—tell me that my job is to feed them, that this is what I get paid to do. So if I don't do this, or if I start doing something else, they're going to leave because they want to be fed. Ouch! Is this what preaching has come to? Are churches now restaurants, with preachers as the chefs? No wonder preaching is one of the main areas where pastors get critiques and compliments!

Viewing preaching as feeding isn't a new concept, because the primary biblical metaphor for pastoring is shepherding. The Greek word for "pastors" in Ephesians 4:11 can be translated as "one who serves as guardian or leader, *shepherd*."[2] In John 10, Jesus, who is the model for pastoral ministry, called Himself the Good Shepherd and used this metaphor to explain how He relates with us, His sheep. In 1 Peter 5, we read that the role of elders (and pastors) is to "shepherd God's flock among you" as undershepherds to the Chief Shepherd, Jesus. And when Jesus was restoring Peter after His resurrection, He did it over breakfast, saying, "Feed my lambs," "Shepherd my sheep," and "Feed my sheep" (John 21:12-17).

So if pastors are shepherds leading their local flocks of sheep, it makes sense that we need to feed the sheep who are under our care. But we must not stop at feeding. We must also engage in "guiding (because sheep easily go astray), guarding (against predatory wolves), and healing (binding up the wounds of the injured)."[3] We must preach in such a way that we are equipping as well as feeding so that the disciples in our churches will grow into "Here I am, Lord" sorts of disciples like Ananias: disciples who see their mission field as the community they are living in. Our churches should be places where the word of Christ is dwelling so richly among everyone that disciples are making disciples by "teaching and admonishing *one another* through psalms, hymns, and spiritual songs, singing to God with gratitude in [their] hearts" (Colossians 3:16, emphasis mine).

How do we do this? It's not by hand-feeding them; shepherds only do that if a sheep is sick. Instead, it's by *equipping them to feed themselves* by leading them to a good grazing pasture! I love how John Stott describes this nuance:

> We who are called to be Christian preachers today should do all we can to help the congregation to grow out of dependence on borrowed slogans and ill-considered clichés, and instead to develop their powers of intellectual

and moral criticism, that is, their ability to distinguish between truth and error, good and evil. Of course we should encourage an attitude of humble submission to Scripture, but at the same time make it clear that we claim no infallibility for our interpretations of Scripture. We should urge our hearers to "test" and "evaluate" our teaching. We should welcome questions, not resent them. We should not want people to be moonstruck by our preaching, to hang spellbound on our words, and to soak them up like sponges. To desire such an uncritical dependence on us is to deserve the fierce denunciation of Jesus for wanting to be called "rabbi" by men (Matt. 23:7-8). . . .

This kind of open but questioning mind is implicit even in the "pastoral" metaphor. Sheep, it is true, are often described as "docile" creatures, which may be so, but they are fairly discriminating in what they eat, and are certainly not uncritically omnivorous like goats. Moreover, the way in which the shepherd feeds them is significant. In reality, he does not feed them at all (except perhaps in the case of a sick lamb which he may take up in his arms and bottle-feed); instead he leads them to good grazing pasture where they feed themselves.[4]

When you preach to equip, you are both feeding and equipping your church since you are leading them to a good grazing pasture where they can feed themselves. This will produce disciples and disciplemakers. But when you preach only as a means of feeding, you aren't equipping disciples to feed themselves. Instead, you are creating a culture of consumerism and overdependence on you.

It's like the difference between eating takeout versus cooking with a meal kit. With takeout, someone else does the cooking and the delivery. So if you feel like eating Korean fried chicken, then that's what you order. Or if you feel like a burger and fries, then you order that instead from another restaurant. You can't really customize the meal once it's been delivered because it's already cooked. And with takeout, you won't get better at cooking or grow in your ability to feed yourself when the takeout restaurant's app doesn't work. As you get older, your skill level will remain the same.

Meal-kit services like Blue Apron and HelloFresh, however, provide you with the recipe and the premeasured raw ingredients. All you have to do is cut up the ingredients and follow the recipe. If you've never cooked a meal in your life, it might take you a bit longer, and the final product may not look exactly like the picture. But if the recipe card says meatballs and rice, you're not going to end up with beef gnocchi. And if you're experienced in the kitchen, you can easily add or take away ingredients to make the meal your own—instead of ginger pork meatballs with bok choy and rice, you may decide that you want teriyaki pork meatballs with mixed vegetables and rice. Regardless of your variation, you're still going to end up with the same core meal as others who ordered the kit—all the while growing in your ability to cook and feed yourself.

When you preach to feed, the church gets to eat a good meal, but no one is learning how to cook (how to read, understand, and apply the Bible). People can obviously deconstruct the meal and try to figure out what the ingredients and recipe were, but it's not the same as seeing it prepared and cooked in front of their eyes. And if the church doesn't know how to cook and feed themselves, then they're either going to show up next week famished, cranky, and malnourished because they haven't eaten all week, or they're going to keep on ordering takeout by watching or listening to sermons from other churches.

Preaching to equip is like offering a meal kit. When you preach to equip, you are helping your church learn how to feed themselves. For example, preaching on the weekend is like opening the meal kit and cooking the first meal of the week in front of everyone and for everyone. You aren't serving up an already cooked meal, but you are taking the ingredients out and showing everyone how to cook one of these meals (how to read, understand, and apply the Bible). And then everyone gets to eat the food! But it's not like going to an all-you-can-eat buffet that leaves you not wanting to see or eat food for the next couple of days. Rather, you're feeding the church with an appropriately portioned, freshly cooked meal, and then equipping them with their meal kits for the rest of the week, so that they can grow in their ability to feed themselves.

Do you see the difference? When you preach to equip, you're preaching to develop, leading your congregation to grow as disciples and equip others as disciplemakers. When you preach to feed, you're preaching to create dependence so that people have to come back next week to eat. Preaching to equip elevates the role of God's word and Spirit to bring about transformation in people's lives. Preaching to feed elevates the role of the preacher and the church service to bring about transformation in people's lives. Preaching to equip is synergistic. Preaching to feed is parasitic. Preaching to equip will produce disciples and disciplemakers. Preaching to feed will produce consumers.

"HERE I AM, LORD"

The great evangelist Billy Graham preached the gospel in person to more than one hundred million people and to millions more through radio and film. Nearly three million people responded to his invitation for salvation.[5] And while his spiritual legacy persists today through his books, his sermons, the schools that bear his name, and the work of his Evangelistic Association, his impact is even greater (and continues to grow) through the millions of people he introduced to Jesus: people who then made disciples, who then made disciples, who then made disciples—most of whom never went to a Billy Graham crusade or listened to a sermon preached by him.

But just think about this for a moment: If Mordecai Ham hadn't said "Here I am, Lord" to Jesus and preached at a series of evangelistic meetings in Charlotte, North Carolina, I wonder whether a sixteen-year-old boy named Billy Graham would have met Jesus. And what would've happened if Billy Sunday hadn't invited Mordecai Ham to speak at those meetings? And if Billy Sunday hadn't learned how to preach by watching John Wilbur Chapman and eventually taken over his ministry, what then? And if Frederick Meyer had never challenged Chapman to respond to God's call on his life, then what? And if D. L. Moody hadn't shared with Meyer's church the story about Edward Kimball leading him to Christ, would Meyer have challenged Chapman? And what would've happened if Edward Kimball hadn't volunteered as a Sunday school teacher? Would he have ever met Moody and had the opportunity to lead him to Christ?[6]

When Ananias said "Here I am, Lord" to Jesus, he never could've imagined that Saul would become an apostle—an apostle who then discipled Timothy, Titus, and countless others. Others who then discipled others, who then discipled others, and on and on. The same is true with Edward Kimball, D. L. Moody, Frederick Meyer, John Wilbur Chapman, Billy Sunday, and Mordecai Ham. They never could've imagined that their "Here I am, Lord" would lead to Billy Graham's "Here I am, Lord," which then led to millions of other people declaring "Here I am, Lord," and on and on.

And thank God that we don't have to worry about all that or try to manufacture it. What pressure! Instead, our responsibility is simple: first and foremost, to do what Ananias did by living a "Here I am, Lord" sort of life. And then to help others do the same. Regular, ordinary disciples making regular, ordinary disciples, leaving the results and impact to God. I think that's doable, don't you?

TEAM DISCUSSION QUESTIONS

1. What was it like placing yourself in Ananias's shoes when you read through Acts 9:1-19? How would you have acted in that situation?

139

2. How do you think Ananias was discipled so that he was able to respond the way he did?

3. When new Christians come to your church, do they tend to be disciples or consumers?

4. Consider your discipleship pathway. In light of this chapter, what sorts of *discover*, *deepen*, and *deploy next steps* can you design to equip the disciples in your church?

5. What changes can you make in your preaching so that people leave equipped and fed, rather than just fed?

Epilogue

From today onward, most leaders

must recognize that the business

they were in no longer exists. This applies

not just to for-profit businesses,

but to nonprofits, and even in certain

important respects to churches.

ANDY CROUCH, KURT KEILHACKER,
AND DAVE BLANCHARD,
"LEADING BEYOND THE BLIZZARD"

WHEN I LOOK OUT THE WINDOW THIS MORNING, I see a fresh coat of snow covering the ground. And while this might stir up memories of Christmas music, hot cocoa, snowmen, snowball fights, and the carefree, gleeful sounds of children sledding, the only sound that I hear is shovels hitting the pavement. I don't hear any children outside. No one is playing in the snow, and no one is excited about it anymore. And that's not because we're a bunch of grinches in Edmonton—it's simply because snow is all we've seen for the last five months.

In case you're wondering, winter doesn't last all year long in Edmonton (and we don't live in igloos), but it is certainly the longest season here. So when it's still snowing in April or May, you can probably guess why children aren't exuberantly rushing outside to play in the snow anymore—as they would if it were the first snowfall of the season. Instead, at this point, everyone's just going through the motions. Forget spring; we want summer!

But for many in 1816, summer never came. In much of the northern hemisphere, that was the "year without a summer." People were stuck in winter because of all the debris in the atmosphere that Mount Tambora had released when it erupted the previous year in Indonesia. One hundred fifty cubic kilometers of ash, pumice, and other rocks, mixed with sixty megatons of sulfur, blocked so much sunlight from getting to the earth's surface that it lowered the average global temperature by as much as 3°C (5.4°F). While this might not sound like a lot, the northeastern United States—more than sixteen thousand kilometers or ten thousand miles away from the volcano—experienced snow and ice in the summer, which destroyed crops, threatening the livelihood of farmers. In Europe, an unusual amount of rain fell, which led to crop failure, which then resulted in famine and disease. And while for the next three years the weather patterns and temperatures in the northern hemisphere were directly affected by the volcanic eruption, the deeper, enduring impact was on people. The disaster affected their social, psychological, emotional, and spiritual health for decades to come.[1]

When the world shut down in March 2020, no one knew for sure what was going to happen. Some saw it as a blizzard that would last a few days or a couple of weeks. Others saw it as a winter that would last a few months. But then there were those like author and thought leader Andy Crouch who, along with his associates Kurt Keilhacker and Dave Blanchard, predicted that it would be like a "little ice age" affecting us for years—if not decades—to come. In their widely shared and profoundly prophetic article articulating all this, they said:

> We're not going back to normal. . . . This time poses the greatest leadership crisis any of us have faced. It can be a moment of amazing creativity, though it also is going to be a time of unavoidable pain and loss. . . . We believe every leader and organization—every nonprofit, every church, every school, every business—should be planning for scenarios that include years-long disruption. From today onward, most leaders must recognize that the business they were in no longer exists. This applies not just to for-profit businesses, but to nonprofits, and even in certain important respects to churches.[2]

Wow. Were they ever right.

Although updates about the vaccine, masks, and shutdowns may feel like a distant memory, years later we are continuing to experience the effects of this "year without a summer" or "little ice age." And as much as we've blamed a lot of things on COVID-19— or used it as an excuse to shut down ineffective programs—if we are being brutally honest with ourselves, I think most of us will admit that everything we're currently experiencing isn't actually because of the pandemic. The pandemic merely accelerated what had already been happening for years in our churches. We were becoming too comfortable with consumeristic practices seeping into the church because of their promised "growth." We were growing increasingly lazy at prioritizing discipleship and creating a disciplemaking culture because we could just rely on disciples transferring into our church. And we weren't effective at raising up evangelists because it was easier if we just shared the gospel while our people did little more than invite others to church.

Reaching today's post-everything world isn't simple. And we can't go back to what we used to do because too many things are different. We are now living in a new world. In fact, I once heard it said that we can know with certainty what has changed, we can know with lesser certainty what won't change, and we can only know with little certainty what will change. So my expectation isn't that this book will be timeless. As culture continues to shift, perhaps the axis in the Interested/Uninterested Matrix will have to change—in fact, I'm 99.99 percent sure that it will need to change. But for the time being, I have found it a useful tool to focus our vision and strategy at Beulah, and I hope you will too in your context.

In the end, the only thing that isn't going to change is Jesus. He is the same yesterday, today, and forever, and He will return as our King. I pray that we will be ready for Him (Matthew 25:13), that we will be found faithful (Matthew 25:23), and that we will snatch as many from the fire as we can (Jude 1:23).

In this post-everything world, how are we to lead our churches to participate more faithfully and meaningfully in the great commission? How can we lead in a way that encourages sleepers to become seekers—and then make the decision to become disciples of Jesus? How can our churches become places where consumers become disciples once again? And where disciples keep on growing to become disciplemakers? I've outlined a framework with principles, ideas, and strategies that I hope are helpful toward that end, but if we don't do what we read in 1 Peter 5, then we won't have a chance. So let me end with Peter's exhortation, encouragement, and prayer for you, for me, and for all our churches:

> I exhort the elders among you as a fellow elder and witness to the sufferings of Christ, as well as one who shares in the glory about to be revealed: Shepherd God's flock among you, not overseeing out of compulsion but willingly, as God would have you; not out of greed for money but eagerly; not lording it over those entrusted to you, but being examples to the flock. And when the chief Shepherd appears, you will receive the unfading crown of glory. In the same way, you who are younger, be subject to the elders. All of you clothe yourselves with humility toward one another, because
>
> > God resists the proud
> > but gives grace to the humble.
>
> Humble yourselves, therefore, under the mighty hand of God, so that he may exalt you at the proper time, casting all your cares on him, because he cares about you. Be sober-minded, be alert. Your adversary the devil is

prowling around like a roaring lion, looking for anyone he can devour. Resist him, firm in the faith, knowing that the same kind of sufferings are being experienced by your fellow believers throughout the world.

The God of all grace, who called you to his eternal glory in Christ, will himself restore, establish, strengthen, and support you after you have suffered a little while. To him be dominion forever. Amen.

1 PETER 5:1-11

Amen.

Acknowledgments

Writing a book isn't just about ideas. If it were, I would've written a few more between this book and my last one! Now don't get me wrong, ideas are important, but I believe what separates good books from great ones is people. People who believe in you. People who will provide you with feedback to make your ideas better. And people who will support you by purchasing a copy and telling their friends about it. So here's my imperfect attempt at acknowledging and thanking all the people who helped this book become a real thing.

Christina, thank you for believing in me when I didn't believe in myself. Your encouragement, love, care, and support gave me the strength and perseverance to get up early on Saturdays and get this done. Victoria, Adelyn, and Makarios, even though you had hoped I'd title this book *No Gold Bullets* or write a fictional children's story instead, being able to write at home with periodic interruptions (and moments of insight) from y'all was a joy and a delight. Dad and Mom Hu, thank you for your library of books that helped me do a literature review on the church growth movement. And Umma, thank you for teaching my children Korean on Saturdays while I was writing!

Dave Schroeder, you are the man! Thank you for being my literary agent and for introducing me to the incredible NavPress team. David Zimmerman and Deborah Sáenz Gonzalez, through this book I'm honored to partner with you, NavPress, and the Tyndale Alliance team to equip and empower the church today to help make disciples and disciplemakers out of the sleepers, seekers, and consumers.

Todd Adkins and Ed Stetzer, can you believe we had already recorded almost five hundred episodes of the *New Churches Q&A Podcast* together by the time the pandemic began shutting everything down? Instead of shutting down the podcast, I'm grateful that we pivoted and recorded approximately one hundred fifty episodes on leading during the pandemic. The genesis of several ideas in this book came out of those conversations. Thank you for the ways that you've sharpened my thinking and contributed to this book.

Beulah staff team, thank you for co-shaping and co-forging many of the ideas in this book together with me in the crucible of life and ministry. I'm so grateful that we get to serve our King Jesus together and be part of awakening Greater Edmonton to Him. Beulah Alliance Church, I love you, I'm honored to serve you, and my prayer is that we would all become regular, ordinary, "Here I am, Lord" disciples like Ananias.

And to every pastor and church leader, don't give up! Yes, we have a common adversary who is prowling around like a roaring lion, looking for anyone he can devour. But Jesus is stronger, wiser, and greater. So let's run with endurance the race that's before us. Let's fight together. Let's always keep our eyes on Jesus. And let's remember whose responsibility it is to ultimately build the church.

Here we are, Lord.

Notes

INTRODUCTION

1. You can watch and read my first words as lead pastor and see how I affirmed my pastoral calling through a pledge here: https://www.danielim.com/2021 /05/20/mypledge.

CHAPTER 1 | THE ASSUMPTIONS WE CAN'T AFFORD TO MAKE

1. There have been hundreds of books written about, from, and out of the church growth movement, so see some of those for a more in-depth explanation of the movement. Here is a glossary of a few pertinent terms:

The church growth movement: "includes all the resources of people, institutions, and publications dedicated to expounding the concepts and practicing the principles of church growth, beginning with the foundational work of Donald McGavran in 1955 [*The Bridges of God*]." Thom S. Rainer, *The Book of Church Growth: History, Theology, and Principles* (Nashville: Broadman Press, 1993), 21–22.

Church growth: "an application of biblical, theological, anthropological, and sociological principles to congregations and denominations and to their communities in an effort to disciple the greatest number of people for Jesus Christ. Believing that 'it is God's will that His Church grow and His lost children be found,' Church Growth endeavors to devise strategies, develop objectives, and apply proven principles of growth to individual congregations, to denominations, and to the worldwide Body of Christ." Donald A. McGavran and Winfield C. Arn, *Ten Steps for Church Growth* (New York: Harper & Row, 1977), 127.

Church growth principle: "a universal truth which, when properly interpreted and applied, contributes significantly to the growth of churches and denominations. It is a truth of God which leads his church to spread his Good News, plant church after church, and increase his Body." McGavran and Arn, *Ten Steps for Church Growth*, 15.

2. McGavran and Arn, *Ten Steps for Church Growth*, 9.

3. C. Peter Wagner, *Church Growth and the Whole Gospel: A Biblical Mandate* (San Francisco: Harper & Row, 1981), 170.

4. McGavran and Arn, *Ten Steps for Church Growth*, 44–45.

5. C. Peter Wagner, *Your Church Can Grow: Seven Vital Signs of a Healthy Church* (Ventura, CA: Regal Books, 1976), 45.

6. McGavran and Arn, *Ten Steps for Church Growth*, 21.

7. Wagner, *Your Church Can Grow*, 189.

8. See, for example, "The Ecological Benefits of Fire," National Geographic Society, updated October 19, 2023, https://education.nationalgeographic .org/resource/ecological-benefits-fire.

9. C. Peter Wagner, *Leading Your Church to Growth: The Secret of Pastor/People Partnership in Dynamic Church Growth* (Ventura, CA: Regal Books, 1984), 46–63.

10. Wagner, *Leading Your Church to Growth*, 63–70.

11. Rainer, *The Book of Church Growth*, 233.

12. Rainer, *The Book of Church Growth*, 234.

13. In Henri Nouwen's book *In the Name of Jesus: Reflections on Christian Leadership* (New York: Crossroad, 1989), he refers to the three temptations that Jesus faced in the desert as the temptations to be relevant, spectacular, and powerful.

14. See Aaron Earls, "Pastors and Churches Face Historic Lack of Trust," Lifeway Research, July 12, 2022, https://research.lifeway.com/2022/07/12 /pastors-and-churches-face-historic-lack-of-trust.

15. Timothy Keller, *How to Reach the West Again: Six Essential Elements of a Missionary Encounter* (New York: Redeemer City to City, 2020), 7.

16. C. Peter Wagner, *Strategies for Church Growth: Tools for Effective Mission and Evangelism* (Eugene, OR: Wipf & Stock, 2010), 30.

CHAPTER 2 | A NEW FRAMEWORK FOR THE NEW OPPORTUNITY

1. Beulah is the name of the church that I have the honor of serving as lead pastor. While our story started in 1907 when the population of Edmonton was about fifteen thousand, we were established as a church in 1921. *Beulah* is a Hebrew word from Isaiah 62:4 that means "married." It's a name that was symbolically applied to Israel and describes the relationship that God wants to have with His people.

2. I deconstructed why we believe this lie (and six other ones) and how it affects our work, life, and love in my book *You Are What You Do: And Six Other Lies about Work, Life, and Love* (Nashville: B&H, 2020).
3. R. Daniel Reeves and Ron Jenson, *Always Advancing: Modern Strategies for Church Growth* (San Bernardino, CA: Here's Life Publishers, 1984), 68–69.
4. John R. W. Stott, *God's New Society: The Message of Ephesians*, The Bible Speaks Today (Downers Grove, IL: InterVarsity Press, 1979), 201.
5. All the names and locations have been changed for privacy reasons, but these are all real stories and people from my Reminders app.

CHAPTER 3 | ESTABLISHING YOUR DISCIPLESHIP PATHWAY
1. If you would like a more comprehensive approach to creating a discipleship pathway, my book *No Silver Bullets: Five Small Shifts That Will Transform Your Ministry* (Nashville: B&H, 2017) can help you.
2. If you would like an in-depth explanation of the eight categories of spiritual maturity, and why these four *ongoing steps* predict greater spiritual maturity, then see chapters 2 and 8 of *No Silver Bullets*. I refer to them as input and output goals in that book.
3. By "bots" I'm not referring to humanoids or lifelike walking and talking robots. I'm referring to artificial intelligence chatbots that you can install and program on your website and/or automatic workflows and processes that you can set up in your church-management system.

CHAPTER 4 | WAKING THE SLEEPERS
1. Daniel I. Block, *The Book of Ezekiel, Chapters 25–48*, The New International Commentary on the Old Testament (Grand Rapids, MI: Eerdmans, 1998), 374.
2. In this study commissioned by Alpha USA, 47 percent of millennials, 27 percent of Gen Xers, 19 percent of boomers, and 20 percent of elders participating in the study—all of whom are practicing Christians—agreed with this statement: "It is wrong to share one's personal beliefs with someone of a different faith in hopes that they will one day share the same faith." *Reviving Evangelism: Current Realities That Demand a New Vision for Sharing Faith* (Barna Group, 2019), 47.
3. In this study commissioned by Alpha Canada, 34 percent of participants strongly disagreed, 19 percent disagreed, 15 percent answered neutral, 17 percent agreed, and 14 percent strongly agreed that "it is wrong to share my Christian beliefs with someone of a different religion or no religion at all, in hopes that they will one day identify as Christian." While 31 percent of Canadian church leaders who participated in the study

said that it's wrong to share their faith with another person in hopes that they will become Christian, Alpha Canada found that 46 to 48 percent of Canadian church leaders who work with children or youth answered much higher, either agreeing or strongly agreeing with this statement. In contrast, 65 percent of senior pastors disagreed or strongly disagreed with this statement. *The Priority and Practice of Evangelism: Canadian Church Leader Perspectives in 2021* (Flourishing Congregations Institute and Alpha Canada, 2021), 18–19. Available here: https://alphacanada.org/lifeshared-2.

4. In this study commissioned by Ligonier Ministries, 27 percent of study participants strongly disagreed, 17 percent somewhat disagreed, 24 percent somewhat agreed, and 32 percent strongly agreed that "it is very important for me personally to encourage non-Christians to trust Jesus Christ as their Savior." *State of Theology* (Lifeway Research and Ligonier Ministries, 2022). Available here: https://thestateoftheology.com.

5. In this study commissioned by the Billy Graham Center for Evangelism at Wheaton College, 8 percent of respondents were very likely, 25 percent were somewhat likely, 26 percent were somewhat unlikely, and 40 percent were very unlikely "to attend church regularly sometime in the future." And 34 percent strongly agreed, 45 percent somewhat agreed, 13 percent somewhat disagreed, 5 percent strongly disagreed, and 3 percent weren't sure that "if a friend of mine really values their faith, I don't mind them talking about it." *Unchurched Report: Survey of 2,000 Unchurched Americans* (Lifeway Research, 2016). Available here: http://research.lifeway .com/wp-content/uploads/2017/01/BGCE-Unchurched-Study-Final -Report-1_5_17.pdf.

6. This was another fascinating finding from the Lifeway Research study commissioned by the Billy Graham Center for Evangelism. They found that of those surveyed (all of whom were unchurched Americans), 73 percent disagree that their Christian friends talk about their faith too much! Five percent strongly agreed, 18 percent somewhat agreed, 31 percent somewhat disagreed, 42 percent strongly disagreed, and 5 percent weren't sure that "my Christian friends talk about their faith too much."

7. In the Lifeway Research study commissioned by the Billy Graham Center for Evangelism at Wheaton College, participants were asked, "Which of the following describes your feelings about the faith of your Christian friends? (select all that apply)." Results were varied: 33 percent responded that they admire it, 18 percent said they put up with it, 14 percent marked that they share it, 13 percent said they ignore it, 1 percent noted they give them a hard time about it, 1 percent said they try to change it, 26 percent said none of these, and 3 percent said they aren't sure.

8. See https://communitychristian.org.
9. Dave Ferguson and Jon Ferguson, *B.L.E.S.S.: 5 Everyday Ways to Love Your Neighbor and Change the World* (Washington, DC: Salem Books, 2021).
10. Sam Chan, *How to Talk about Jesus (without Being THAT Guy): Personal Evangelism in a Skeptical World* (Grand Rapids, MI: Zondervan Reflective, 2020), 8.
11. Here's how Sam Chan describes plausibility structures: "We all have plausibility structures that determine whether a story is unbelievable or believable. These plausibility structures are essentially preprogrammed and predetermined inside us. . . . Where do these plausibility structures come from? Three main sources contribute to our plausibility structures: (1) community, (2) experiences, and (3) facts, evidence, and data. . . . Which is the most powerful source in determining belief? You might assume it's facts, evidence, and data. Maybe you desperately want it to be facts, evidence, and data. But facts, evidence, and data are actually the least powerful in determining belief. . . . So which is the most powerful in determining belief? Community. The term *community* refers to friends and family we know, love, and trust. Community is the most powerful force in determining belief. Community shapes the way we interpret our experiences. Community shapes the way we interpret facts, evidence, and data." Chan, *How to Talk about Jesus*, 2–4.
12. Chan, *How to Talk about Jesus*, 8.
13. Chan, *How to Talk about Jesus*, 9.
14. Rosaria Butterfield, *The Gospel Comes with a House Key: Practicing Radically Ordinary Hospitality in Our Post-Christian World* (Wheaton, IL: Crossway, 2018), 13–14.

CHAPTER 5 | WELCOMING THE SEEKERS

1. *Unchurched Report: Survey of 2,000 Unchurched Americans* (Lifeway Research, 2016). Available here: http://research.lifeway.com/wp-content/uploads/2017/01/BGCE-Unchurched-Study-Final-Report-1_5_17.pdf.
2. John Stott, *Between Two Worlds: The Challenge of Preaching Today* (Grand Rapids, MI: Eerdmans, 1982), 329.
3. In this study commissioned by Alpha USA, non-Christians were divided into two groups: those who identify with a faith other than Christianity ("religious non-Christians") and those with no faith at all ("atheists/agnostics/nones"). Religious non-Christians answered that they would be more interested in Christianity if Christianity had better evidence to support it, if Christianity had a better reputation, and if they saw various churches in their community working together more. Atheists/agnostics/

nones answered that they would be more interested in Christianity if Christianity had better evidence to support it, if Christianity had a better reputation, and if they had an eye-opening spiritual experience themselves. *Reviving Evangelism: Current Realities That Demand a New Vision for Sharing Faith* (Barna Group, 2019), 23.

4. In the same study, 30 percent of non-Christians said that they would like to explore faith through a casual one-on-one conversation, 23 percent through a casual conversation within a group, 20 percent through a person at church, 7 percent through a video/movie, 6 percent through a concert venue, 5 percent through a tract, 3 percent through a person on the street, and 41 percent through none of these. *Reviving Evangelism: Current Realities*, 58.

5. In this study commissioned by Alpha USA, 42 percent of non-Christians completed the sentence "I would be more interested in learning about Christianity and what it could mean for my own life if" with "the Christians I know were less judgmental of my personal beliefs." Other answers included "the Christians I know were less judgmental of my lifestyle" (37 percent), "the Christians I know were more welcoming and hospitable" (31 percent), and "the Christians I know were more humble and aware of their shortcomings" (30 percent). *Reviving Evangelism in the Next Generation: United States* (Barna Group, 2021), 31.

6. In this study commissioned by Alpha Canada, 27 percent of non-Christians completed the sentence "I would be more interested in learning about Christianity and what it could mean for my own life if" with "the Christians I know were less judgmental of my personal beliefs." Other answers included "the Christians I know were less judgmental of my lifestyle" (27 percent), "Christianity had better evidence to support it" (23 percent), and "I had an eye-opening spiritual experience myself" (20 percent). *Reviving Evangelism in the Next Generation: Canada* (Barna Group, 2021), 31.

When asked, "Which environments would you be open to attending or participating in?" 25 percent of unchurched self-identified non-Christian teens in the US said an "in-person, one-on-one conversation with a friend," 17 percent said a "digital, one-on-one spiritual conversation with a friend," 16 percent said an "online church service, by myself," and 14 percent said an "in-person church service, with someone else." *Reviving Evangelism in the Next Generation: United States*, 35.

7. When asked, "Which environments would you be open to attending or participating in?" 17 percent of Canadian unchurched self-identified non-Christian teens said an "in-person, one-on-one conversation with a friend,"

11 percent said a "digital, one-on-one spiritual conversation with a friend," 8 percent said an "in-person church service, with someone else," and 7 percent said an "online church service, by myself." *Reviving Evangelism in the Next Generation: Canada*, 35.

8. Stott, *Between Two Worlds*, 326.

CHAPTER 6 | CHALLENGING THE CONSUMERS

1. A. W. Tozer, *The Tozer Pulpit: Volume 3* (Harrisburg, PA: Christian Publications, 1970), 37.
2. Eugene H. Peterson, *Working the Angles: The Shape of Pastoral Integrity* (Grand Rapids, MI: Eerdmans, 2000), 97–98.
3. Peterson, *Working the Angles*, 2.
4. I wrote an article defining echo chambers and their relationship with discipleship and the discipleship pathway. You can find it here: https://www.danielim.com/2017/11/07/echo-chambers-discipleship.
5. Chad Walsh, *Campus Gods on Trial* (New York: Macmillan, 1962), 102.
6. Leonard Sweet, *Rings of Fire: Walking in Faith through a Volcanic Future* (Colorado Springs: NavPress, 2019), 190–192.

CHAPTER 7 | EQUIPPING THE DISCIPLES

1. F. F. Bruce, *The Book of the Acts*, rev. ed., The New International Commentary on the New Testament (Grand Rapids, MI: Eerdmans, 1988), 189.
2. Frederick William Danker, *A Greek-English Lexicon of the New Testament and Other Early Christian Literature*, 3rd ed. (Chicago: University of Chicago Press, 2000), 843.
3. John Stott, *Between Two Worlds: The Challenge of Preaching Today* (Grand Rapids, MI: Eerdmans, 1982), 120.
4. Stott, *Between Two Worlds*, 177.
5. Marshall Shelley, "Evangelist Billy Graham Has Died," *Christianity Today*, February 21, 2018, https://www.christianitytoday.com/ct/2018/billy -graham/died-billy-graham-obituary.html.
6. If you would like to learn more about the chain of events that led to Billy Graham's conversion, look up "Edward Kimball to Billy Graham" on Google.

EPILOGUE

1. See *Encyclopaedia Britannica Online*, s.v. "Mount Tambora," https://www.britannica.com/place/Mount-Tambora; Becky Little, "The Deadliest Volcanic Eruption in History," HISTORY, January 16, 2018,

https://www.history.com/news/the-deadliest-volcanic-eruption-in
-history; and Robert Evans, "Blast from the Past," *Smithsonian Magazine*,
July 2002, https://www.smithsonianmag.com/history/blast-from-the
-past-65102374.

2. Andy Crouch, Kurt Keilhacker, and Dave Blanchard, "Leading beyond the
Blizzard: Why Every Organization Is Now a Startup," *The Praxis Journal*,
March 20, 2020, https://journal.praxislabs.org/leading-beyond-the
-blizzard-why-every-organization-is-now-a-startup-b7f32fb278ff.

About the Author

Daniel Im is the lead pastor of Beulah Alliance Church, a multi-generational, multiethnic, and multicampus church in Greater Edmonton, Alberta, Canada. He has written several books, including *You Are What You Do: And Six Other Lies about Work, Life, and Love*; *No Silver Bullets: Five Small Shifts That Will Transform Your Ministry*; and (with Ed Stetzer) *Planting Missional Churches: Your Guide to Starting Churches That Multiply*. He cohosts the *IMbetween Podcast* with Christina, his wife, which helps listeners discover the tools to build a marriage and family they love. He also serves as a Bible teacher for *100 Huntley Street*, Canada's longest-running daily television show.

Daniel has an MA in global leadership from Fuller Theological Seminary and has served and pastored in church plants and multi-site churches ranging from one hundred to fifty thousand people in Vancouver, Ottawa, Montreal, Korea, Edmonton, and Nashville. Because of their love for the local church, after pioneering and leading the church multiplication initiative for Lifeway, Daniel and Christina moved back to Canada in 2019 with their three children.

As a Gallup Strengths Performance Coach (Strengths Advisor), Daniel has led over six hundred people through the CliftonStrengths assessment (formerly known as StrengthsFinder) in multiple countries. He is a scholar-practitioner who can not only create theories but also implement them in innovative ways to solve problems. His experience and strength are in fostering alignment and momentum within teams and churches by employing strategies and systems to move the church toward multiplication. You can read more about Daniel and invite him to speak at your event at danielim.com.

Also by Daniel Im

You Are What You Do:
  And Six Other Lies about Work, Life, and Love

No Silver Bullets:
  Five Small Shifts That Will Transform Your Ministry

Planting Missional Churches:
  Your Guide to Starting Churches That Multiply (with Ed Stetzer)